WHAT TOP-PERFORMING SALESPEOPLE DO DIFFERENT

WHAT TOP-PERFORMING SALESPEOPLE DO DIFFERENT

10 Proven Strategies to Level Up Your Skills
and Close More Sales

L'areal Lipkins

Copyright © 2023 L'areal Lipkins

The information provided in this book is for general informational purposes only. The author and publisher make no representations or warranties of any kind regarding the accuracy, completeness, suitability, or effectiveness of the strategies and techniques discussed. The success of these strategies may vary based on individual efforts, market conditions, and other factors. The reader is solely responsible for their actions and decisions based on the information in this book. This book is not a substitute for professional advice. Always seek the advice of qualified professionals regarding financial, legal, or business matters. The author and publisher disclaim any liability for any loss or damage caused by the use or reliance on the information provided in this book.

What Top-Performing Salespeople Do Different / L'areal Lipkins
ISBN: 979-8-9872015-0-3
www.LarealLipkins.com

Printed in the United States of America

This book is dedicated to my dad who passed away during the writing process. Thank you for kicking me in the butt and reminding me to always finish what I start.

It has been a journey to finish this book, but we did it!

I love you, always!

"We must overcome the notion that we must be regular. It robs you of the chance to be extraordinary and leads you to the mediocre."

Uta Hagen

CONTENTS

INTRODUCTION

This book has been years in the making...13 years, to be exact!

For a long time, I thought about writing a sales book sharing my insights after training thousands of salespeople, but the timing never seemed "right."

Then 2020 came along and completely disrupted life, business, and sales as we knew it. We're a few years removed now, but how we sell has changed more in the last three years than in the past 30 combined.

There's been a shift.

And long gone are the days of Rolodexes and pushing products.

If you believe that sales is about wheeling and dealing, arm-wrestling people into a yes, or manipulating people into buying something they don't want or need, you will be disappointed with this book.

While those old approaches might have worked in the past, that doesn't align with my philosophy about sales, nor is today's buyer willing to put up with that outdated approach to solving their problems. Today's buyer is savvy, has more information, and can easily find an alternative solution with a quick Google search.

So, *now* is the perfect time to release this book because the demand for high-performing salespeople has never been higher in today's competitive business environment.

And as organizations embrace digital transformation, adapt to new selling models, and usher in the next generation of salespeople, there is a hunger and eagerness to learn from those who consistently achieve outstanding results.

So, what *is* this book about?

After training over 10,000 salespeople, it's relatively easy for me to identify who will do well in sales and who will struggle.

At first, I thought it was just my gut instinct or experience. However, as I started to anaylze the differences between top performers, average performers, and underperformers, it became overwhelmingly clear that being successful in sales isn't random.

There are specific habits, characteristics, and mindsets that help top-performing salespeople consistently operate at such a high level.

In other words, regardless of where you are in your sales career right now, you can learn how to become exponentially better if you do what top performers do.

In this book, you'll learn the top 10 behaviors you need to succeed in B2B sales, regardless of what you're selling, your years of sales experience, or what's happening with the economy.

This book is not meant to be an exhaustive list of all the things top performers do differently. Narrowing the list down to only 10 beliefs, habits, or tactics was more challenging than writing the book, because different selling environments have nuances.

With that said, my goal was to focus on the tools that met these three characteristics:

Consistency: I've regularly seen it be a differentiator between top and average performers, regardless of experience, price point, or industry.

Ease of implementation: Everything you will learn is relatively easy to incorporate into your sales approach and process. And this doesn't mean that some of your old paradigms won't be challenged because they will!

Greatest ROI: This is not a rah-rah motivational sales book. Everything included in this book is immediately actionable and will help you close sales faster and easier if you use it.

Who is this book for?

This book is for you if:

- You're in your first *real* sales job and trying to figure out what in the world you just signed up for. We've all been there ... Welcome to the club!

- You've been selling for a couple of years, and you're doing "okay," but you know if you want a long-term career in sales, you need to set the correct foundation.
- You're hitting your numbers consistently, but always looking for ways to improve your sales skills.
- You're a veteran, but you've realized that some of the hardball or traditional sales tactics you've used in the past aren't working as much, and you need some modern sales tools.
- You lead or manage salespeople and you're trying to identify how you can best support their development.

How to get the most out of this book

First, I suggest determining what you want from reading this book. I know that might be weird, but when I'm reading a personal or professional development book, I find it helpful to think about what I want to gain from it.

Maybe you want to sharpen your skills, perhaps you feel stuck in a rut and need something to light your fire again, or maybe you need a reminder to stop complicating things and get back to basics. Whatever you'd like to get from reading this book, write it down.

Next, stay coachable. It is more likely than not that I'm going to say something that creates some internal resistance. Sometimes we feel resistance because we're unsure how to apply what we just learned in our unique selling environment. I've trained salespeople in dozens of industries, including SaaS (software as a service), digital marketing, recruiting, financial services, advertising, biotech, consulting, legal tech, commercial janitorial, pest control, commercial real estate, construction, corporate event planning, HVAC, audiovisual, aviation, IT, and industrial parts.

So, everything I cover in the pages that follow will apply. It may require modifying it to fit your personality or process, but it still applies and works. But determining how to best use it in your world is up to you.

Other times we feel resistance because our beliefs have been challenged, and we like to hold on to our old beliefs because they make us feel safe. The problem with that mindset is that growth doesn't happen when you're in your comfort zone, and the beliefs that got you here (in your sales career), won't get you there (where you want to be).

Know that resistance is a sign that your paradigms are being stretched to meet the new level of performance you desire and are capable of.

Lastly, implement what you learn. One of the best practices I picked up from a conference I attended years ago is to create a top 10 list. You do this by going to a blank page in the book (or a journal) and writing numbers 1 thru 10. You'll use this list to write down your biggest ahas or specific actions you commit to taking. I find my top 10 lists far more helpful than just highlighting a bunch of things because it helps me prioritize my takeaways and creates action steps for me. Plus, it gives me a quick list to review if I ever want to go back and reread a book.

As you're reading through the chapters and learning new methods to help with your sales, I would love to know some of your key takeaways. If you feel compelled to share something you found valuable or if you have a question, email me at Lareal@LarealLipkins.com.

Alright, the time is here! Let's get you on the path to closing more sales and making more money!

Chapter 1

MASTER YOUR MINDSET

"The hallmark of successful people is that they are always stretching themselves to learn new things."

Carol S. Dweck

Can we have an honest conversation? I know that "mindset" has become a personal and professional development buzzword over the last couple of years. And for a long time, I too thought it was just a fluffy concept.

But after training over 10,000 salespeople and sales leaders, I can say with 100% conviction that mindset is hands-down the most important part of being a high-performing salesperson.

Yes, your sales mindset is more important than any sales tactic, technique, or strategy you will ever learn. In fact, your mindset is even more important than having the best product, price, or sales process.

I know that's a bold claim, especially from someone whose business is sales training and consulting.

But it's true.

None of those things matter if you don't know how to control the thoughts that are running through your mind every day.

Let me explain...

My first five years as a sales trainer, I spent a lot of time teaching the sales methodology—I taught at the time—which was heavily focused on sales tactics and techniques. Week after week, dozens of salespeople would come to our training sessions, learn the lesson for the day, and they'd go back into the field. It didn't take long to realize that most of our students were soaking up the knowledge, but not actually applying what they were learning.

Even when I would have a 1:1 coaching session, I'd quickly recognize that their issue wasn't skillset, it was mindset.

They were scared to apply what they were learning, so they kept doing what they were doing, even though it wasn't working.

They were afraid of rejection and failure, so they never picked up the phone.

They were afraid of the prospect saying, "No!" So, they'd settle for a wimpy, "I'll think it over."

They were uncomfortable talking about money, so they'd present a proposal without talking about the budget.

This isn't a coincidence. There is an underlying cycle at work, and it keeps salespeople from achieving their goals. Once you understand this phenomenon, you can use it to your advantage.

Let's look at what's happening below the surface.

Your beliefs drive your behaviors, and your behaviors determine your results.

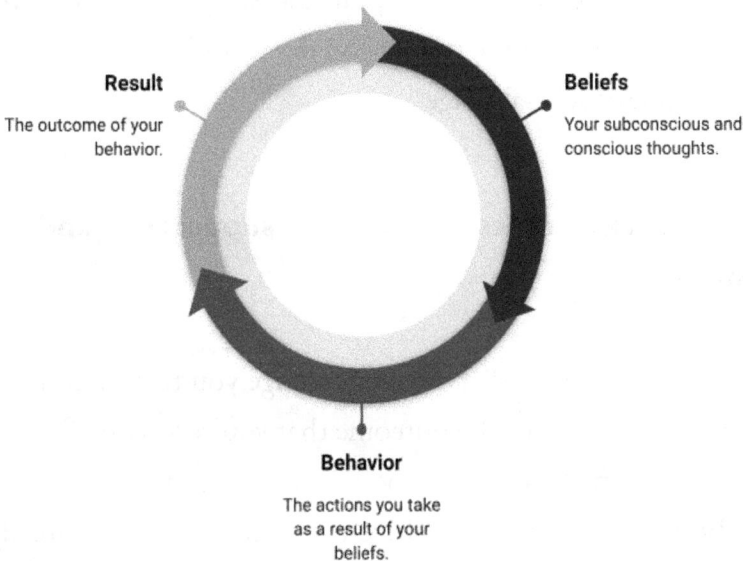

Result
The outcome of your behavior.

Beliefs
Your subconscious and conscious thoughts.

Behavior
The actions you take as a result of your beliefs.

BELIEFS

Your beliefs represent your thoughts, perspective, and what you believe to be true. According to Dr. Fred Luskin of Stanford University, people can have up to 60,000 thoughts a day. That means that everything you do—in sales and life—is first driven by a thought. If you have a busy day running errands and think it's going to rain, you'll likely take an umbrella, wear a jacket, or park close to the entrance. If your prospect is straightforward in their communication style and you're not, you may think you need to rush the process, so you ask fewer questions and skip a step or two. It doesn't matter what the behavior is. Everything you do is driven by some thought and those thoughts reflect your beliefs.

Of the 60,000 plus thoughts you have every day, approximately 80% of these thoughts are negative, and 90% of them are repetitive. That means that if you're not intentional about your thoughts and beliefs, you will continue to repeat the same behaviors, even if they're not getting you the results you desire and are capable of. We call this a cycle of self-sabotage.

There are two types of beliefs: supportive and non-supportive.

Supportive beliefs are beliefs that encourage you to take action that aligns with your goals or the outcome that you're looking for. When you have a supportive belief about something, it's easier to take action because you have a positive perspective about it already. A great example of this is if you are naturally inquisitive and curious. You will likely enjoy asking prospects a lot of questions during the discovery and qualification phase. It's like a treasure hunt for information that you can then leverage throughout the sales process.

However, if you think asking people too many questions is intrusive or you're scared of ticking the prospect off, then you will likely avoid asking probing questions because it makes you uncomfortable and you assume it makes the prospect uncomfortable, too. This would be a non-supportive belief. Non-supportive beliefs keep you from taking the action that aligns with your goals or the outcome you're looking for. Non-supportive beliefs are often driven by negative past experiences, fear of rejection, insecurity, lack, and false assumptions.

BEHAVIOR

Behavior is the action you take or that you don't take. Remember, your behavior (what you see) is driven by your beliefs (what you don't see), so just like there are supportive and non-supportive beliefs, there are supportive and non-supportive behaviors.

Asking for referrals, continuing to make calls even when you encounter a rude prospect, and spending five minutes to research a prospect so you can warm up a call, are all supportive behaviors. On the other hand, presenting a proposal before you've fully qualified a prospect or spending hours "researching" a prospect to avoid prospecting are non-supportive behaviors. It's important that you're doing the right behaviors because your behaviors will determine your results.

RESULTS

Results are the outcomes. In sales, there are macro-outcomes, like whether you closed the sale, hitting your quota, or calling the enterprise target account that's in your territory. Macro outcomes are the big things that most salespeople and sales leaders focus on improving because they're typically tied to sales metrics. However, what many salespeople and sales leaders don't realize is that macro-outcomes are the result of micro-outcomes.

Micro-outcomes are the small results like gathering more information on the sales call, because you asked more questions, or being able to hit the ground running on Monday, because you did all your research on Friday. Micro-outcomes are easy to bypass, because you don't immediately see how they improve your sales performance. But the compound effect of micro-outcomes is huge and leads to macro-outcomes.

Additionally, micro-outcomes help build your confidence and momentum. Instead of saying I need to increase sales by 10% this year, which is a **macro**-outcome, you can focus on a **micro**-outcome that can help you do that. A simple micro-outcome could be asking two additional questions during the sales process that help you identify additional gaps that can be filled by a higher-level product/service (upselling) or a complementary product/service (cross-selling). Either way, instead of focusing on getting more deals, you can focus on asking better questions to increase your average deal size to achieve your 10% growth in sales revenue.

Why is this important?

Understanding the relationship between your beliefs, behavior, and results is paramount because when you're not getting the results you want (not hitting quota, getting beat up on price, prospects ghosting you, etc.), what's the first thing you try to change?

Quite frankly, if you're like 99.9% of most salespeople and managers, then the first thing you will try to change is your behavior. Let's use the example that once you present your proposal, prospects keep telling you that your price is too high, and it's keeping them from moving forward.

Most salespeople will either go to their sales manager and try to sell them on why they need to give the prospect a discount. Or maybe they'll try to overcome the objection by telling them all the additional value they're getting for the price. They may even read some sales book that gives them a foolproof script they will attempt to use.

The problem with all of these options is that they don't address the underlying issue. If the prospect is saying the price is too high *after* the proposal is presented, that means the salesperson didn't talk about the budget before putting the proposal together. And while those solutions may work in the short run, they're not sustainable or the habits of top-performing salespeople. The salesperson will unnecessarily find themselves back in that situation again.

The real problem could be:

- They're skipping the budget conversation because they're uncomfortable talking about money.
- They're afraid that if they ask about the budget, the prospect won't tell them, or they'll think they're going to take them for all they have.

- They're not asking enough questions to uncover their pain and hidden motivators because they don't want to offend the prospect or risk making them upset.
- They don't believe in the company's pricing, and it shows when they present their proposal.
- When the salesperson makes a purchasing decision, price is a big factor for them, so they struggle to sell value.

By the way, these aren't just random examples. These are the behaviors and mindsets that I've seen when coaching salespeople. That's how I know that a script, even the best one, won't help you if you're not sold on the price first or you're uncomfortable talking about money. In the heat of the moment, you will either forget to use the script or you'll use it, but you won't execute it effectively. Either way, you won't get the outcome you want.

OUTGROWING YOURSELF

One of my favorite quotes about human potential and mindset is from Archilochus. Archilochus was a Greek lyric poet and soldier who once said, *"We don't rise to the level of our expectations, we fall to the level of our training."* And while I believe that to be undoubtedly true, it can also be said that ...

We don't rise to the level of our expectations, we fall to the level of our mindset, because your mindset will always trump your skillset.

That doesn't mean that you don't try to change your behavior. What it *does* mean is that you also must change the belief that is driving the behavior if you want the behavior to be maintained. Otherwise, you'll constantly be chasing the next sales tactic.

Here's the thing: You achieve success at the level of your beliefs and top-performing salespeople have top-performing beliefs.

But that doesn't mean that they don't have any negative beliefs.

What they do have is a higher awareness of their beliefs, and how they impact the way they show up. They believe in themselves and their ability to figure things out. They are willing to lean into discomfort because they see the discomfort as a sign of growing versus a sign that they should stop or give up.

Working on your mindset is a never-ending journey, not a destination. I remember when I transitioned from marketing to sales, and I had multiple self-sabotaging beliefs:

- I'm not a salesperson.
- Sales is about manipulation and trying to convince people.
- I'm reserved and introverted.
- I'm too young; no one will take me seriously.

I thought that once I got my first sale that all those negative beliefs would go away. But the reality is that landing my first sale unleashed a whole new set of negative beliefs.

- It was only $3,500.
- I don't know if I can close the backend business.
- What if I was just at the right place, right time?
- That was too easy; it's too good to be true.

Even when I started setting different milestones: $10k, $25k, $50k, $100k, $250k, etc., I thought my mindset would be magically fixed, but it wasn't. The only solution was to become more intentional about taking control of my thoughts and changing my mindset.

One of the questions I often get when I host my Master Your Mindset Workshop for sales teams is, "How do I know what beliefs are holding me back?"

Below is a list of some of the most common self-limiting beliefs that I've seen working with salespeople. As you read through the list, highlight or underline any non-supportive beliefs that resonate with you.

- I have to be the cheapest to get the deal.
- I am too young; no one will take me seriously.
- I have to be the "expert," so that means I need to have all the answers.
- They don't want to talk to me.
- They probably don't need any help.
- I haven't been in the industry long enough to call them.
- It's rude to ask about their budget.
- I don't want to be too pushy.
- I need this sale.

- The prospect is in control of the conversation.
- If they like me, they'll eventually buy from me.
- The economy is down, and no one has any money.
- I can't sell anything because operations can't deliver it.
- I need to educate the prospect, so they see me as an expert.

The beliefs you highlighted are the beliefs you want to start working on reframing. If there are additional beliefs you know are holding you back, but they weren't on the list, write those down as well.

Remember your beliefs drive your behavior which determines your results. So, the second way you can determine your non-supportive beliefs is to identify where there's a gap in the results you're currently getting and the results you want.

Here are some examples:

Current Result	Desired Result
Average sales cycle is 45 days.	Average sales cycle is under 30 days.
I keep getting stuck at the gatekeeper, and never get to speak with the decision maker.	I have more conversations with decision makers, so I can book more quality appointments.
Average deal size is $5,000.	Double average deal size to $10,000.

Notice the chart has both macro results, like sales cycle and price of the offer, as well as micro results, like getting stuck at the gatekeeper. Once you make your list, pick one that you want to focus on, and you can reverse engineer what's happening to identify the underlying beliefs. In this example, we'll pick average deal size so you can see how the process works.

Current Result	Current Behavior	Current Belief
Average deal size is $5,000.	I'm only presenting the lowest offer. I'm only presenting one offer instead of selling a bundle or comprehensive solution. I'm focused on the product that I think will be the easiest to sell, even if I know they would benefit from additional services.	$10,000 is a lot of money to ask someone for. Some money is better than no money. I've only been here six months, so I don't have enough experience to sell the higher- end services. If I try to sell the largest package, they may say, "No" to everything, and I won't hit my quota.

For this process to be effective, you must be honest with yourself. Additionally, you might find there's several behaviors or beliefs that are contributing to one result, and that's normal.

If you struggle to pinpoint some of the beliefs that are below the surface, the three debriefing questions you will learn in Chapter 10: Debrief Your Calls will help you.

MINDSET BUILDERS

I personally don't like books that tell you everything you need to fix, but they don't give you any practical ways to fix it. With that said, I want to be part of the solution and share six ways you can build and maintain a healthy mindset.

1. **Debrief your calls**. Listening to your sales calls is so powerful that I've dedicated an entire chapter to it. In Chapter 10, you'll learn how to use debriefing to elevate your mindset and your sales skills.

2. **Journal**. Journaling is an easy way to get your thoughts out of your head and on to paper. Seeing them written down makes it easier to address, because it gives your ideas and thoughts a place to live outside of your head.

3. **Set goals.** Setting goals gives you something to work toward, and it keeps you focused on the end goal. We'll dive more into how to set goals properly as a salesperson later.

4. **Check-in.** I'll be the first to admit that this is going to sound a little kumbaya-ish, but it's been a game-changer for me personally. Throughout the day, I do mindset check-ins where I'll take a few minutes to become aware of my

thoughts. *How am I feeling? Is there anything I'm procrastinating on?* Why? Checking in with myself helps to slow me down and ensure that I'm not falling into the 90% repetitive thought cycle.

5. **Be selective**. Stay away from other salespeople who are always negative and complaining about the company, quota, commission, customers, or product. It's hard to maintain a positive mindset when you're surrounded by negativity, because before you know it, you'll be complaining too.

6. **Own your development.** Reading books like this one is a great way for you to learn different ways of thinking and being. You can also go to events, take a course, attend an online training, listen to a podcast, do a sales call audit, or join a community of people who have similar goals. The key is that you shouldn't rely on your company as your sole source of professional development. You are your biggest asset, so you should be investing in yourself.

The way we do business is constantly changing due to new technology, economic conditions, politics, regulations, and social norms. But the one truth that remains the same is that you must master your mindset first in order to improve your sales performance. Therefore, if you want to thrive in any selling environment, not only do your behaviors have to adapt, but the way you think must change, too.

Chapter 2

SET GOALS THAT STICK

"You have to set goals that are almost out of reach. If you set a goal that is attainable without much work or thought, you are stuck with something below your true talent and potential."

Steve Garvey

You may be thinking, "What does setting goals have to do with being successful in sales?"

Well, let's look at the data.

According to a study by CEB (now Gartner), sales representatives who received formalized goal setting and coaching outperformed those who did not by 17%. A second study by Matthews and Saylor found that salespeople who set specific goals increased their sales performance by 30% compared to those who did not set specific goals.

Unfortunately, most companies are so focused on teaching product knowledge and figuring out the latest tool to add to their tech stack that they don't teach their salespeople how to set goals that drive long-term personal and professional growth. But the reality is that ...

Salespeople grow in the direction of their goals.

That means if you want to get to the next level in your sales career (or life), you have to set goals that make you stretch beyond your current comfort zone. The best goals are the ones that require you to do something different or better than what you're already doing—which is when growth happens. This also means that you're going to have to change some of your current beliefs because the beliefs that have gotten you to this point in your sales career won't get you to the next level of your career, which is why we talked about your mindset in Chapter 1.

Since we grow in the direction of our goals, if you don't set any goals, you'll continue to be where you are today. And when you set goals that are too small, you run the risk of selling yourself short of your actual potential. Now this is fine if you're happy with the success you've achieved so far, and you don't want more. But if you know you are capable of more, it all starts with defining what "more" looks like.

In this chapter, we're going to focus on setting personal and professional goals. Understand that setting goals is a lifestyle, not a one-time event— like most people think. When you approach it from the lifestyle perspective, it's much easier to think about goals that matter to you.

You can set goals for everything:

- Your day. What do you want to accomplish today?
- For a sales call. What do you want to accomplish by the end of this call?
- For reading this book. What do you want to get out of reading this book?

The more you start thinking about the outcomes you're looking for or the needle you want to move, the more focused and intentional you become about how and where you invest your time.

GOALS DEFINED

Now before we dive too deep into how to set goals as a sales professional or sales leader, let's agree on a common definition of goals. When I'm doing goal-setting workshops for sales teams, salespeople often think I'm talking about their quota or annual budget, and this is not the case.

For clarity, your quota is a goal, but it's a goal that is likely given to you by your company and probably isn't the main reason why you get up every morning. The type of goals I'm talking about are meaningful personal and professional ones that light a fire under you. This includes the dreams you want to accomplish, the experiences you want to have, the items you want to buy, the awards you want to win, the organizations you want to be able to support, the lifestyle you want to provide for your family, and the person you want to become.

Top-performing salespeople understand that having meaningful goals helps them:

- Stay motivated.
- Level up their skills and activity.
- Push through fear and discomfort.
- Bounce back from rejection faster.
- Focus on the right behaviors.
- Manage their time, energy, and effort.

Your goals are what will keep you going when you're doing the work, but not seeing the immediate results. Your goals are what will help you make one more call, even when no one is answering. Your goals are what will give you the guts to call the CEO on the phone versus hiding behind email.

Think about it this way...

What's your level of patience when you're working a sales opportunity in February versus December? In February, you're probably a lot more accommodating and patient because it's still the beginning of the year. But if you're like most salespeople, you're a bit scrappier and braver in December. Why? Because you have a number to hit, and you don't have time to waste.

What would happen if you had the same mindset and focus the entire year? My guess is that you wouldn't be desperate to hit your quota at the eleventh hour.

HOW TO SET GOALS THAT MOVE THE NEEDLE

Here are six steps to get you started on setting goals like top-performers.

Figure out what you want.

This is the most important, and oftentimes, the most difficult part of setting goals: getting crystal clear about what you want. I find most people (salespeople and non-salespeople alike) are so busy living their lives day-to-day that they don't stop long enough to think about what they are working toward or what success looks like for them.

I know it can be overwhelming trying to decide how and where to start, but you don't need to figure out your whole life right now. Plus, there are no good or bad goals. It's all about what motivates you to get up in the morning and help you show up for yourself every single day.

When I do goal-setting workshops, I have the salespeople start by picking three goals they want to focus on achieving in the next 90 days. Three goals are easy to manage without getting distracted or discouraged. The reason we aim for 90 days is because 30 days can feel too short to build momentum, and a year can feel too long to stay motivated. So, a quarter gives you enough time to make progress while also allowing you to modify your goal or plan if you need to.

Lastly, as you think of your three goals, I recommend picking two professional and one personal. I like having both personal and professional goals because you are *more* than just a salesperson.

You have other roles that you play and other interests outside of what you do professionally, and they deserve your attention, too.

Write down your goals.

According to a study conducted by Gail Matthews, a psychology professor at Dominican University, you are 42% more likely to achieve your goals just by getting them out of your head and on to paper.

Why? Because writing your goals down challenges you to clarify what you say you want. A goal can sound good in your head, but when you write it down, you might realize that it needs to be more specific or that you need to break it down to a smaller goal given your timeline.

Seeing your goals on paper also helps you to assess what challenges you may face working toward them and to gauge whether or not it's a goal that you're fully committed to.

When you start to ask yourself questions like, "How am I going to do that?" or "Where am I going to find the extra time?" it's tempting to find the answer right then and there. But don't focus on the "how" right now, just keep your attention on writing down three goals you're committed to achieving in the next 90 days.

Create a plan to achieve your goal.

The next step is to create your action plan for the goals you've written down on paper. I've found the easiest way to do this is to brainstorm all the steps you need to take or milestones you need to reach and then add a deadline to each one to hold yourself accountable.

For example: Let's pretend it's September and your goal is to achieve President's Club before the end of the year. When you take a look at your numbers, you need to generate $250,000 in sales to make the cut.

Some potential action steps could include:

- Review what you currently have in your pipeline to see what deals you can close.
- Set up next steps with all your open opportunities and strategize how to get the deal over the finish line.
- Reach out to current customers who might need additional products or services.
- Ask current customers, who don't need additional products and services, about referrals or making introductions.
- Reach out to old customers and prospects that are already familiar with your company and see if it makes sense to re-engage.
- Create a target list of prospects and do a prospecting blitz.

Obviously, you don't have to do all of these steps, but brainstorming narrows down the list to a handful of things that you believe are most likely going to get you to your goal.

As you make your plan, you want to avoid a big mistake that people make: creating a plan with rose-colored glasses. When you make your plan with rose-colored glasses, you create it in a perfect-world scenario that doesn't exist. As a result, when you start to execute your plan, you're likely to hit some roadblocks that you didn't even consider but should have. And when that happens, it is easy to get derailed and never follow through.

I don't want that to happen to you, so think of potential roadblocks upfront. For the President's Club example, a potential roadblock could be that you only have 90 days, but your average sales cycle is 120 days.

How can you address that?

Maybe focus on smaller deals that you can close faster, or you can review your sales process and see how you can optimize it.

There's no right or wrong answer. The point is that when you think about potential roadblocks or constraints ahead of time, you can build a better plan.

Create a routine.

I know you may be thinking, "Didn't we just do that?" But there's a huge difference between having a plan and having a routine. Your plan is your individual task list of all the things you need to do to accomplish your goals, but your routine is something you're going to do on a consistent basis. For example, using the same goal from earlier, you might create a routine of asking three people a week for a referral or introduction or prospecting two hours every day, Monday through Friday. Routines will help you stay on track vs. starting off motivated and then slowly losing steam.

Take action.

Now, it's time to execute your plan and routine. Warning: This is where fear and those old beliefs will start to creep back up and try to keep you from doing the things you need to do. The only way to get past the fear is to go through it, so challenge yourself to take action, even if you're scared.

Track and monitor your progress.

Create a weekly check-in with yourself where you can reconcile what you planned to do and what you actually got done. Fridays are a great day to do this because you can close out your week and plan for the next week. As you're monitoring your progress, you may notice that you need to adjust your plan based on new information or perhaps you ran into a challenge that you didn't foresee, and that's okay.

On the flip side, everything may be going as planned and firing on all cylinders. The purpose is to have regularly scheduled check-ins to hold yourself accountable as you move forward with your goals.

GET THE JUICES FLOWING

Hopefully your wheels are turning right now and you're thinking about why you do what you do, the life you want to create, and the impact you want to make as a sales professional. But if you're feeling stuck, there's two things I always recommend my clients do.

One, block off an hour of quiet time where you can sit and think. I personally like to do this outside because the sound of nature relaxes me, but do whatever works for you.

Ask yourself the following questions to help you decide some potential goals to focus on:

- What specific achievements or milestones do I aspire to reach in my sales role?
- How do I define success in my sales career, both in terms of numbers and personal fulfillment?
- What skills or areas of expertise do I want to improve or acquire to excel in my sales career? How can I proactively work on developing these skills over time?
- What experiences do I want to have personally or with my family?
- Fast forward a year from now, what are some things I want to say I've done?
- Where is there a gap in certain areas of my life?
- What legacy do I want to leave behind in terms of the relationships I've built and the problems I've solved?

The second thing you can do is go through the process with your spouse. A few years ago, I had a client tell me he really didn't need to make any more money because he had done well for himself. I reached in my desk and gave him a goal-setting packet to complete with his wife, feeling pretty certain that she had some things she'd like to put on the list. We both laughed at his response, and the following Monday he showed up 10 minutes early for class. He was so giddy that he looked like a five-year-old boy that had a secret he just couldn't hold anymore. My client told me that that was the first time in 20 years that he and his wife had ever really talked about goals, much less set goals together.

He started sharing all the goals they had come up with, but there was one that stood out to me. When he and his wife started having children, she left her career to be a stay-at-home mom. While she enjoyed that, she also wanted to be more than "just a mom." With their youngest soon finishing up high school, she wanted to either start a business or go back to work. His wife had never told him how she felt before, but the goal-setting process gave them space to have the conversation. That's powerful!

I'd like to end this chapter with a quick exercise showing you what happens when you set goals.

Put your index finger up like you're making the number one. Next, hold your index finger about two inches from your nose at eye level. Stare at the tip of your finger for five seconds and notice what happens.

What you will notice is that as you focus on the tip of your finger, everything else around you will become blurry. That's what happens when you're clear about your goals and you're intentionally taking action every day to reach them. It's time to bring your priorities and goals into focus and eliminate all the other distractions like the economy, competitors, and office politics. *Besides, at the end of the day, you can't control any of those anyway.*

Now that we've set a good foundation by covering mindset and understanding the importance of setting goals that propel you forward, let's get into some tactical things that top-performers do *differently* to consistently exceed their numbers.

Chapter 3

KNOW YOUR NUMBERS

"If you can't measure it, you can't improve it."

Peter Drucker

One of the most notorious quotes in sales is that "**sales is a numbers game**." And these words of wisdom are usually weaved into some motivational spiel or sales management soapbox moment, trying to encourage salespeople to *just* get in front of more people.

But the harsh reality is that if sales is *just* a numbers game, most salespeople are losing before they even start.

What do I mean?

Unfortunately, most salespeople don't actually *know* what their numbers are, and if they do know their numbers, they don't know how to use them to improve their performance.

If you want to consistently hit your numbers and win the game of sales, there are three different numbers that you need to track. They will assist you in focusing your time, energy, and efforts on the tasks that matter most instead of getting in the weeds and growing frustrated.

Top salespeople track at least two if not all three of these numbers while average salespeople *might* track one.

THE BASICS: BEHAVIOR

The first number or metric you want to track is your behaviors. Your behaviors are the activities that you need to do on a consistent basis to get on the phone (or face-to-face) with someone who can purchase your products or services.

The exact behaviors you need to track depends on your specific industry, but some common ones are:

- Number of dials
- Number of referrals asked for
- Number of quality conversations at a networking event
- Number of prospecting emails that you send out
- Number of LinkedIn requests you make or messages you send

What do you notice about these behaviors?

They are all actions that are directly within your control. You can control how many dials you make, referrals you ask for, and LinkedIn messages you send. This point is incredibly important for you to grasp.

The more you regularly track these activities, the easier it will be to maintain a funnel of qualified prospects. A lot of salespeople, especially those who manage the full sales cycle (prospecting to close), get so busy managing their active opportunities that they stop prospecting.

When that happens, their funnel dries up and they find themselves in a cycle of feast and famine. Not only is this extremely discouraging, but it's also easily avoidable by ensuring you're hitting your minimum level of behaviors consistently.

Even if you have sales development reps (SDRs) or business development reps (BDRs) that support you in keeping the top of your funnel full, you still have behaviors you can (and should) track on repeat. For example, you can track the number of referrals you ask for or the number of old prospects you reach out to.

Notice that I didn't just mention the behavior. I also added an amount to that behavior. If your company gives you a target level of activity, let's say 10 LinkedIn outreaches a week, then that should be your baseline. However, if your company hasn't given you a target level of activity, you can take two approaches. First, you can go ask your sales manager what that number should be based on what successful salespeople are doing. Or you can look at what you've averaged over the last 90 days to give you a benchmark. Commit to hitting your benchmark for the next 90 days, track the results, and then re-evaluate after 90 days to see if you need to change your activity level.

There is a huge misconception that tracking behaviors is only for newbies. While tracking your behaviors is important if you're brand new at the company or new to sales, because there's a lag between doing the behaviors and closing a deal. Top-performing salespeople *still* track their behaviors because they know if they're not doing their behaviors consistently, it's going to negatively impact their pipeline 30-60 days later.

RED FLAGS: LEADING INDICATORS

The second number you should track is your leading indicators.

Your leading indicators are the results of your behaviors. Suppose that one of the behaviors that you are tracking is the number of dials, then the leading indicator you might track would be the number of appointments that you are booking from those dials.

Or if you'd like another layer of data, you can track the number of dials, the number of conversations you're having, and the number of appointments you're booking.

The more data you have, the easier it is to pinpoint what piece of the sales process you need to improve.

I once had a client, Deanna, who was fearless on the phone, and she was good at connecting with people. The problem was that she didn't have a prospecting plan and was trying a little bit of everything. I had listened to her calls before, and I knew that's where she should spend the bulk of her time. We had a conversation, and I asked her to commit 80% of her prospecting time to the phone.

After 30 days of tracking her behaviors in her case dials, Deanna was able to determine that 1 out of 8 people she called turned into an appointment. She was shocked! She only needed to make 80 dials a month to book 10 appointments.

Can you imagine how empowered you would feel knowing exactly what you needed to do to hit your numbers?

The powerful idea about tracking more data is that you can easily identify where the gap is occurring and close it faster. If you have a goal of five new appointments per week (leading indicator) and you're making 100 dials per week (behavior), but you're only booking two appointments a week, the first number you can look at is the number of conversations you're having.

You may discover that you are making enough dials, but you're not having enough conversations, and therefore, you need more dials. Of course, there are other factors you can consider like what time you're calling, who you're calling, and how you can leverage email and social media in addition to hopping on the phone, but for the purpose of this example, let's keep it simple. Let's pretend after looking at the data, it's clear that you are in fact having enough conversations. The breakdown can actually be what you're saying during your conversations to convert more people to an appointment.

But, you don't know, if you don't know your numbers.

Aside from appointments, other leading indicators to consider are:

- Referrals received
- Site visits
- Talk time
- # of appointments
- # of demos
- # of proposals
- % of appointments kept

There is a driving force in being able to know your numbers and knowing which leading indicators that you need to fine-tune.

In addition to being able to see where your gaps are, tracking your behaviors and leading indicators allows you to adjust early on. You no longer have to wait until the end of the month or end of the quarter to know whether or not you're hitting your numbers, because your leading indicators will let you know if you're on or off track. As a result, you can make any necessary changes and course-correct much sooner, rather than later.

HISTORY: LAGGING INDICATORS

The third and final number that you need to track are your lagging indicators.

Your lagging indicator metrics are determined from your leading indicators. Most likely, these are the numbers that you and your boss are already tracking.

Lagging indicators may include:

- Quota attainment
- Revenue generated
- Profit margin
- Average deal size
- Sales cycle
- Close ratio
- Number of new clients
- Customer acquisition cost

To better understand the overall effectiveness of your lagging indicators, look at more than one. You might have a good close ratio, but you realize that your sales cycle is twice as long as the company's average. That might be an indicator that there's room to shorten your sales cycle or that the other people are rushing the process. Maybe you have a high win rate, and you always achieve your quota, but your profit margin is low because you're using discounting to get the deal. By looking at multiple lagging indicators, you can get a more accurate view of what's really going on and fix it.

A few years ago, a Dallas-based financial services company contacted me to coach one of their sales reps. Usually, companies contact me to coach a rep because they're underperforming, but this wasn't the case. This rep was consistently hitting his quota, so when I met with him, I asked if he knew why the company wanted him to work with me, given he was always at the top of the leaderboard. His exact response was, "Because I burn through opportunities, and every month I have to start over." The good news is that he was self-aware!

The sales reps were supposed to do 60% new business, 40% account management. In other words, more than half of their revenue should come from new logos or accounts, and the balance should come from existing accounts they were continuing to nurture and support. In our interaction, I could tell that nurturing and supporting wasn't natural for him.

He wasn't interested in checking in or maintaining the relationship with his prospects. He was a hunter and liked the thrill of the new deal. His motivation was to get new logos, and this rep was good at it. I took a closer look at his account breakdown (lagging indicators), and I could see that less than 20% of his revenue came from existing accounts, but he was far outpacing everyone on new appointments and accounts. If I had only looked at quota attainment or the number of new logos, I would have thought he was doing great. However, reviewing his account breakdown and retention gave me a completely different story. Or should I say, it gave me the *complete* story?

After our conversation and looking at his numbers, it was clear that even with training and coaching, this rep was never going to be exceptional at account management. Not only that, but it's much easier to find an account manager than an innate hunter. So, the CEO and I decided that it was best to hire an account manager who could support his clients and the sales rep would come back in for quarterly reviews and renewals. Six months later, this top-ranking rep was crushing his sales numbers, his clients were taken care of, and the company was happy because revenue was up.

It isn't just about tracking data for the sake of tracking data. It's about using the data to make improvements.

WHAT IS THE DATA TELLING YOU?

Recently, I was working with a mid-market company that does digital marketing for associations.

With over 200 salespeople, one of their biggest challenges was shortening the ramp-up time for new hires. The first step we took was to evaluate their sales leaders to see what they needed to do differently to manage, coach, train, and develop their sales team.

The second step was to evaluate their metrics.

As we studied the dashboard, I could instantly see a difference between the top performers and the bottom performers. Normally, you would think that the top performers were doing more activity than the bottom performers, but in this case, that wasn't true. The top performers actually made less calls than bottom performers.

However, they had a longer average talk time and more opportunities created. This means they were having longer, higher quality conversations with prospects versus smiling-and-dialing, and therefore those conversations were converting to opportunities at a higher level.

This is why it's mandatory to not only track the data, but to review it regularly to clearly see the story the information is telling you.

- Where are most of your leads coming from?
- What metric do you need to focus on improving?
- Where are you getting stuck in the process?
- Do you do better selling certain products or services?
- Is there a subconscious money threshold that you have?
- Are your calls too long?
- Are your calls too short?
- At what point does the probability of you closing a deal go down?

By the way, if you're thinking, *I'm too busy to do all that*, you're not thinking like a top performer.

Average salespeople think that this is the sales manager's job, and the only time they look at the numbers is when they already know that they're behind or they're having a one-on-one with their sales managers. And that's too late.

Top performers don't bury their heads in the sand. They want to get 1% better every day because they know small incremental changes lead to huge payoffs. They obsess about their numbers, because they know the numbers will reveal exactly what's going on and how to get in a position to win. The numbers will highlight which parts of the sales process need to be tweaked, instead of simply thinking that getting in front of more people is the best move.

Sales is *more* than a numbers game, and to be a top performer, you need more data.

GETTING STARTED WITH METRICS

Before we wrap up this chapter, I want to make sure you have a clear roadmap moving forward. Here is a cheat sheet to refer to that will have you knowing your numbers like the back of your hand.

Identify Your Metrics

Know what your behaviors, leading indicators, and lagging indicators are that make sense for your role and business. By focusing on all three levels, you can really dive deep into figuring out how you can be more effective as a salesperson, but also more efficient with your sales process.

Track Your Metrics

If your company has a CRM (customer relationship management) or some type of customer dashboard, use it!

Average salespeople think the CRM is just a system for their manager to see if they're doing their job or simply software to store your customers info, but it is a powerful tool for you, if you know how to leverage it.

One of the main benefits of using the system is that you can clearly see your metrics. Your metrics will tell you where you're losing money and what areas you need to fix.

If your company doesn't have a CRM, you can create an Excel spreadsheet.

Create a Cadence

Come up with a rhythm of how often you're going to look at your metrics. This will be determined by your sales cycle as well as how many opportunities you're working at any given time. An extremely high-volume transactional industry will require you to be looking at your numbers on a daily basis. On the other hand, I have a client in the aviation space where they only bring on a few new clients per quarter, so they're looking at their numbers on a bi-weekly basis.

Look for the Story

What story are the numbers telling you? If you read between the lines, it can guide you in pinpointing specific changes that you're going to make either in the behavior or the amount of activity you're doing.

In the end, the type of activity that you're doing or the effectiveness of your behaviors and activities can increase the chances of you closing more business.

Chapter 4

KEEP YOUR PIPELINE FULL

"Consistency is what transforms average into excellence."

Atul Gawande

If you look at a funnel, you will see it is larger at the top and then it gets smaller at the bottom. Your sales funnel works the same way. At the top of the funnel, you have a large amount of people and prospects, and as they work their way through your sales process (which we'll talk about in the next chapter), the number of people who continue will gradually get smaller.

At the smallest end of the funnel is your actual pipeline. While your funnel consists of all the opportunities you have, your pipeline is focused on the deals that have the highest probability of closing within a specific timeframe.

Either way, it's important to understand that your pipeline is part of your funnel, but they're not one and the same.

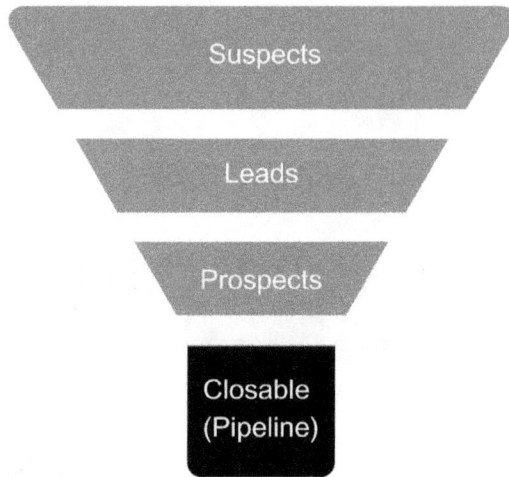

Top-performing salespeople know that managing their funnel and pipeline is critical to their sales success.

First, it's imperative to keep your pipeline full because it provides a constant flow of potential customers, opportunities, and revenue instead of being on the revenue rollercoaster where you have one really good quarter and then the next quarter your numbers drop.

Salespeople who master the art of keeping their sales pipeline full are better equipped to achieve their targets and drive consistent growth.

Secondly, a full pipeline helps you forecast revenue more accurately. At the individual rep level, you can better assess your workload, prioritize prospects, and allocate resources based on the volume and quality of opportunities in your pipeline. And on an organizational level, accurate forecasting allows organizations to align their sales strategies, set realistic targets, and allocate resources accordingly.

A full sales pipeline also offers better visibility into the sales process. You can track leads as they progress through different stages, allowing you to identify potential bottlenecks or areas of improvement. This clarity helps you analyze historical data, identify trends, and adjust your strategies and resources.

MORE OPPORTUNITIES, MORE CONFIDENCE

One of my favorite things to do with my clients is sales call audits. A sales call audit is when they send me a link to a recording of a real sales call to review. After listening to how they run the call, I put together a detailed report of what they did well, what they could have done differently, and then we review it together.

Based on the conversation, I can tell if the salesperson has a healthy or dry pipeline.

When your pipeline is full, you're a better salesperson because you're not desperate to close every deal. In other words, keeping your funnel full gives you plenty of options. You ask better questions, you address red flags, because you're more emotionally objective.

On the flip side, when it's the end of the month and you only have two opportunities, needing to close both to earn commission, then there's a good chance that you're wheeling-and-dealing and overly anxious to close the sale.

GOOD OL' PIPELINE HYGIENE

In the previous chapter, we talked about knowing your numbers and doing your behaviors consistently to keep the top of the funnel full. And in this chapter, I'll give you the strategies that top performers use to keep their funnel and pipeline full of prospects. But first, I want us to be clear about something.

There is a difference between keeping your pipeline full and keeping your pipeline bloated.

When your pipeline is **full**, it's filled with quality and qualified prospects who have the capacity and ability to purchase from you. With these opportunities, you've uncovered a gap that your product/service can close. You know you're talking to the people. You've talked about money and timeline. You know there is a high probability that you will be able to convert those prospects into paying clients within the next 30 days. If your sales cycle is less than 30 days, then your pipeline would be deals you expect to close in less than 14 days.

However, when your funnel is **bloated,** it's congested with unqualified opportunities that you're pretending are real opportunities. In other words, you're lying to yourself and your boss about the probability of conversion. And while it takes off some of the pressure when you're reviewing your pipeline with your manager because your pipeline *looks* good, it will come back to bite you at the end of the month when the deals don't close, and you're having to explain what happened, or should I say, why it didn't happen.

We often say that time is money, but time is infinitely more useful than money because you can always make more money, but you can't make more time. And high-performing salespeople understand this concept, so they know that it is in their best interest to let deals go that are not likely to convert versus continuing to invest more time and energy, only to get no ROI. Holding onto low-quality opportunities doesn't serve you, the prospect, nor the company.

KEEPING YOUR PIPELINE FULL, NOT BLOATED

It all starts with what happens at the top of your funnel.

Remember, your funnel is all the opportunities you're working on, while your pipeline are the deals you should be closing in less than 30 days, depending on your sales cycle.

Let's talk about the concept of having a "full" pipeline, because it's relative depending on your numbers, sales cycle, and sales effectiveness.

For example, let's say that you and I work for the same company, and we both have a monthly quota of $250,000 in new business. If you have a 70% close ratio, you need to have $357,142 worth of opportunities in your pipeline to meet your numbers. On the other hand, if I have a 30% close ratio, I need $833,333 worth of opportunities. I'm going to either need more or larger opportunities than you to meet the same number. Obviously, over time, I can improve my sales skills to increase my close ratio, and I don't have to have as many opportunities in my funnel to hit my goals. Once again, this is why it's so imperative that you know your numbers.

Depending on what CRM your company uses, you should be able to pull a report to see how many opportunities you need to have at each stage of your sales process or at least overall to consistently hit your numbers. *(You can also use an Excel spreadsheet in lieu of a CRM.)*

All you'll need to do is review the deals you've closed over the last 6-12 months to see your average deal size, average sales cycle, and close ratio. From there you can determine how much you need in your funnel.

If you're supported by a sales development rep (SDR) or business development rep (BDR), then it's primarily their responsibility to set appointments for you. However, if they're not generating enough appointments, you will likely need to do some prospecting. If you own the full sales cycle, then you already have to book your own appointments and it's critical that you laser in on the behaviors we mentioned in the last chapter.

To increase the number of people that enter the top of your funnel to keep it full (and consequently your pipeline full), here are three methods to consider. Depending on your role, prospects, and organization, some of these will be a better fit than others.

REFERRALS AND INTRODUCTIONS

When's the last time you got a referral or introduction to a potential client?

If it's been more than 90 days, this is an area that you really want to prioritize. According to *Top Sales World Magazine*, salespeople who actively seek out and exploit referrals earn 4 to 5 times more than those who don't.

Referrals and introductions are extremely effective as they serve as a third-party endorsement, lowering your prospect's guard and making them more likely to have a conversation with you. As the marketplace becomes noisier and your prospects have more options, referrals and introductions will be your go-to sales strategy.

You may have noticed that I'm using the terms *referrals* and *introductions* and that's because they're two different approaches to gaining prospects. A referral is when someone gives you another person's name. *Melissa, you should reach out to Jared over at ABC Company because they're having the same issues as us, and I think you can help them.* Or it can happen in reverse where you tell Jared that he needs to reach out to Melissa at 123 Enterprises because they helped you solve a similar problem.

While referrals are better than nothing, I always prefer to get an introduction because it's far more effective and adds a personal touch. Instead of just telling you to reach out to this person or have someone pass your information along, an introduction actually connects you to a prospect, typically through email or in person, and it is easier to book appointments.

Now think back to that last introduction or referral you received.

Did you ask for it, or did someone happen to make it an unsolicited referral or introduction?

There's nothing wrong with receiving a referral voluntarily, but think about how many *more* referrals or introductions you could get if you simply asked for them.

How convenient would it be if you were able to get one more quality referral or introduction a month? What about two? Five?

My point is that both referrals and introductions can help you sell smarter, but you must ask for them. According to a survey by Dale Carnegie, 91% of customers say they'd give referrals, but only 11% of salespeople ask for them. Even if you don't get one on the first ask, it subconsciously makes the person more aware of potential referrals and introductions they can make in the future. Although it's not an immediate win, it's planting seeds that can take root and pay dividends in the future.

Networking events, professional associations, and online communities are other excellent avenues to expand your referral network. By tapping into these connections, you can access high-quality leads with a higher chance of conversion.

SOCIAL MEDIA

Social media is no longer about posting breakfast photos and cat videos, but it can be incredibly effective in making you visible in front of ideal, potential clients.

To make the most of your time, you want to choose platforms that align with your target audience, whether it's LinkedIn, Twitter, Facebook, Instagram, or even TikTok.

Regularly share valuable content, new trends, and industry news to position yourself as a knowledgeable and trusted expert. Actively engage with your audience by responding to comments, answering questions, and participating in relevant conversations.

When it comes to B2B sales, my ideal client is on LinkedIn, so I've made a commitment to showing up on LinkedIn consistently. Every time I post, I either get a testimonial from a client sharing a win in my comments, someone joins my email list, another person signs up for one of my courses, buys a book, sets up a call, or likes my post, and it gets shared with their audience— all of which adds more potential prospects to my funnel and builds compound interest over time.

The other way I use social media is for direct outreach. I actually booked a contract with a company that does over $800 million in annual revenue by sending a personalized message on LinkedIn. In my email, I introduced myself, created a connection by referencing a mutual contact, clearly stated why I was reaching out to her, and inquired about next steps. It wasn't fancy, but it was effective ... and profitable.

There are several ways to leverage social media and build relationships online that can lead to warm leads and referrals.

- Connect with prospects, decision-makers, and industry influencers in your target market.
- Engage with their posts, share their content, and provide thoughtful comments.
- Show a genuine interest in their work and industry challenges.
- Use direct messaging to start conversations and establish connections.

PROACTIVE PROSPECTING

We can't talk about keeping your pipeline full without mentioning good ol' fashion prospecting. Successful salespeople engage in proactive prospecting to continually fill their pipeline with potential leads.

First things first, you need to define your ideal customer profile (ICP). Take some time to understand who your perfect customer is—their industry, demographics, pain points, and goals. This clarity will help you narrow down your prospecting efforts and target the right people.

Once you know who you're looking for, it's time to do some detective work. Research and identify potential leads using tools like

LinkedIn, industry directories, or grassroot networking. Dig deep and find those individuals or companies that align perfectly with your ICP.

Now comes the fun part: personalized outreach.

This can involve cold calling, cold knocks, networking, asking for referrals/introductions, direct outreach on social media, and email outreach.

Regardless of which channel you use, you want to make sure you craft tailored messages that speak directly to your prospects' pain points and show them how your product or service can solve their problems. Be genuine, make it clear that you've done your homework (this also warms up your interaction), and let them know you're there to help.

Remember the contract I secured with a large enterprise client from one LinkedIn message?

Proactive prospecting isn't dead, it just requires a little more effort and strategy.

Don't stop at the first contact. Follow-up is the secret ingredient to building genuine relationships and keeping prospects engaged. Be persistent, but not pushy. A well-timed phone call, a thoughtful email, or even a personalized video message can make all the difference.

And remember, proactive prospecting isn't a one-time event. Continuously track and measure your results, and fine-tune your approach based on what works best. Refine your strategies, experiment with different channels, and adapt to the ever-changing needs of your prospects.

Maintaining a full pipeline makes you more confident on calls, gives you more data points, and ensures consistent revenue and commission, making it easier for you to achieve your sales goals. By being proactive and taking the initiative, you'll most certainly keep your sales pipeline overflowing with promising opportunities.

Throughout this chapter, we identified strategies to achieve and sustain a full sales pipeline, and in the next chapter, we will explore the secret to consistent sales.

Chapter 5

FOLLOW A SALES PROCESS

"Without a process, success is just a matter of luck."

George Doran

A few years ago, I was working with a salesperson for an industrial parts start-up. He had worked relentlessly in this position for about 18 months, but struggled to bring new vendors on.

The CEO reached out to me to do sales coaching with him. However, as he shared what was going on internally, there was a strong indication that the reason he was struggling was because he lacked a sales process to follow. So, I suggested that I meet with the salesperson first to ask some questions, and then I would come back to the CEO with my recommendations.

During my conversation with the salesperson, my suspicions were confirmed. I shared with the CEO that instead of doing coaching or training, the first step we would take is to build an actual sales process. Then, we could do coaching and training around the process that we developed. He agreed, and I spent the next week learning their business and building out a step-by-step sales process to bring on new vendors. I walked the leadership team through the sales process, we made a few changes, and then I trained the salesperson on the process.

Prior to working together, it was taking them 71 days on average to bring on a new vendor. After putting in a step-by-step sales process, the next deal they closed only took 17 days, and the one after that was just 14 days!

How did we shorten the sales cycle by 80%?

We identified what needed to happen at each stage of the process and put in the proper steps *within* each stage. By training the salesperson, I ensured he had the skills and scripts to execute the process on his own.

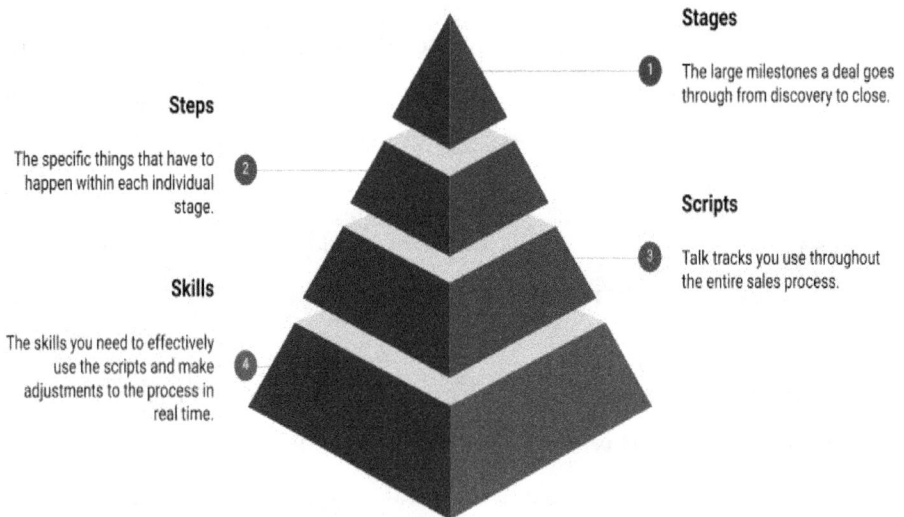

Stages

1 The large milestones a deal goes through from discovery to close.

Steps

2 The specific things that have to happen within each individual stage.

Scripts

3 Talk tracks you use throughout the entire sales process.

Skills

4 The skills you need to effectively use the scripts and make adjustments to the process in real time.

Let's define what a sales process is so we can make sure we're working from the same definition.

A sales process is the stages and steps you go through to consistently convert a qualified prospect to a paying client.

It is a roadmap that guides you through each step of the sales cycle, from initial contact with a prospect to closing the deal. It helps you stay organized and focused on the most critical tasks and provides a consistent approach that you can improve over time. When you follow a sales process, you can move prospects through the pipeline more efficiently and effectively, increasing your chances of closing more deals.

In other words, a sales process is your blueprint that tells you what you need to do next.

Most companies *think* they have a sales process in place, but all they really have are generic stages: Prospect, Discovery, Qualification, Present Proposal, Negotiate. While it's a start, it's only a quarter of the process and one of the reasons why most salespeople are underperforming and end up doing their own thing.

At the end of one of our first coaching sessions, I asked the industrial parts salesperson the same question I ask every client, "What was your biggest takeaway?"

He let out a long sigh as if he had been holding his breath the last 18 months. "Everything," he said. That's not surprising to me.

Sometimes people respond that way because they're still processing *everything* we covered during the coaching session. But I could tell from the look of relief on his face that when he said "Everything," he actually meant it.

He then shared more insight about what he was walking away with.

He said that before we started working together, he felt like he was alone in a dark room with his hands tied behind his back trying to find his way around, but then I came in with a flashlight and directed him on a path to follow.

I was speechless.

Not only did it move me as his coach, but I think it is a profound analogy that unfortunately describes the way a lot of salespeople feel behind their desks.

When you don't have a sales process in place, it can be incredibly frustrating when you're hard-working but you're not yielding the results that you want.

Selling doesn't have to feel like you're in an escape room, trying to decipher clues, find hidden doors, and solve riddles.

Your sales process is your cheat code.

Sidenote: If you manage the sales team and you don't have a documented sales process that consists of stages, steps, scripts, and skills, this is the first place you need to start.

TOP-PERFORMING SALESPEOPLE DON'T WING IT

Top-performing salespeople follow a sales process, because they don't want to waste a lot of time jumping through hoops. They want the easiest path to closing the deal. In addition, they know that in today's world, where buyers have access to more information than ever before, having a sales process is not an option, it's a necessity. Structure and organization is brought to your sales approach, helping you to better understand your prospects' needs, and making your life a whole lot easier.

Mediocre or average salespeople don't like following a sales process. They believe that every sales opportunity that they're working on is unique. They frown at the thought of following a process, because they think they perform better "on the fly," and they see a sales process as being too rigid. Salespeople, who fall in the "average" category, rely on their personality, but the truth is that your personality is only going to get you so far.

Processes scale, personality does not.

Oh, and if you're thinking *I know a salesperson that does well and they don't follow a process, they're just naturally good at sales,* chances are, if you *really* watch them, you'll notice they have their go-to phrases, tactics, questions, responses, and client stories. This is their unique sales process that they've curated over time and may not have been formally written down.

When the sales process is designed and executed correctly, it should reduce common roadblocks and shorten the sales cycle. But that's just scratching the surface. Here are five reasons to make sure you have a sales process that is optimized for conversions:

Clarity

A sales process provides you with a step-by-step framework to follow. You can clearly identify where a prospect is at any given point in time, and what it is that you need to do to move them to the next step. Your sales process is vital, because it allows you to manage multiple opportunities at one time without feeling overwhelmed. It allows you to track where you are getting stuck, giving you a chance to come up with a strategy to get the deal moving again. Not having a sales process to refer to will have you all over the place trying to manage deals, and you will be lost because you won't know what is or is not working.

Control

Your sales process allows you to maintain control, knowing the exact stages and steps that are needed to take the prospect through, and when you want to do each step. Let's assume a prospect wants to talk about budget, but you haven't had a chance to even do a proper discovery. When you have a good sales process established, you're able to acknowledge their desire to know about the budget, but then take back control by setting the expectations that you will get to the budget *after* you understand what their specific needs are. But this confidence in redirecting your prospect comes from knowing your process. If you don't have one you may often feel the pressure to follow the prospect's lead and lose control of the call.

Competence

Your competence or skill level is sharpened thanks to your sales process. You will do the same process repeatedly, instead of recreating the wheel every time you're working an opportunity. Secondly, as you build your competence, you'll be able to make slight adjustments to how you apply the process in real-time, so that it fits the context of the opportunity that you're currently working.

Confidence

Competence builds your confidence. The more you execute your process, the more confident you will become at what comes next, knowing you're not starting from scratch every time. Can you imagine being able to anticipate and address potential roadblocks before they come up? What about having your go-to questions that work every time on cue? Or having a talk track for the common questions prospects ask versus having to come up with an answer on the spot? That's what your sales process allows you to do. When you have a proven sales process that works, you can rest assured that if you follow the process, the desired outcome will happen.

Conversions

Lastly, you want to make sure that your sales process is optimized for conversions. This means it's designed to address or eliminate common roadblocks. Failing to have your sales process optimized for conversions, will have you jumping over hurdles, chasing prospects, offering to discount your price, finding out about hidden decision-makers, and presenting too early before you actually created the value.

COMMON SALES PROCESS MISTAKES

Now that you see why your sales process is a huge component to your long-term success, let me share with you three common mistakes to avoid.

Mistake #1: Not personalizing the process.

Just because you have a sales process, doesn't mean you have to follow it rigidly. In fact, it's the opposite.

> **When you master your sales process,
> it gives you more flexibility.**

How can a process give you more flexibility?

Because when you're clear about where you are in the sales process at all times, if your prospect tries to skip ahead, you *realize that they're skipping ahead* or they're out of the process altogether. Without a process, you don't know whether or not they are bouncing around and if you answer their questions, you don't know where you need to get back to.

Keep in mind that every prospect is unique and has different needs, so it's important to tailor how you execute the process to make it feel natural. It will be slightly different if I'm meeting directly with a CEO vs. meeting with a VP of sales that needs to "sell" the idea of working with an outside consultant to the CEO. Although the process is the same, the execution is different because the situation is different. Average salespeople either don't have a sales process in place or when there's a curveball, they don't know how to adapt the process in real-time.

Your sales process isn't about checking off each step and pulling the prospect through the process. It's about guiding the conversation to its destination.

Mistake #2: Skipping steps.

So, you're eager to close the deal and you think you can shortcut the process by bypassing steps? Bad idea!

Every step in your sales process is there for a reason, and skipping any of them can harm the overall effectiveness of the process and come back to bite you. There are a couple of scenarios where I see this happen more frequently:

- When the pressure is on at the end of the month and salespeople are trying to get a deal in.
- When it's an existing client
- When salespeople oversell something trying to get the deal done
- When the buyer is more assertive than the salesperson and they don't like confrontation.

When you pick and choose which steps to take, you will slow down the process on the backend or create an operational nightmare when they become a client. Don't be tempted to cut corners. Take your time and be carefully guided by each step.

Mistake #3: Not understanding the prospect.

Every prospect has needs and pain points that your sales process will reveal to you. But if you're just going through the motions and not taking the time to really listen to what they're saying, you're not going to be able to provide the solutions they need.

Take time to really understand your prospect's needs, goals, desires, and challenges, and you'll see a big difference in your success rate.

You can now take the mystery out of sales, because when you have a sales process that works and that you implement consistently, you have the cheat code that makes sales simple, fun, and financially rewarding.

Chapter 6

DO A PRE-CALL PLAN

"It's the little details that are vital.
Little things make big things happen."

John Wooden

Bracing myself, I buckled my seat belt.

"So, walk me through the plan for your first call," I told the sales rep I was doing a full day of "ride-alongs" with.

She looked at me with a nervous smile and replied, "We'll see!"

"We'll see?!" I repeated, hoping that she was merely joking.

She wasn't.

I was doing ride-alongs with this rep to determine where she needed training and coaching. Within five minutes of our day, I already had the first item on my list that we needed to target—a pre-call plan.

Unfortunately, this isn't a one-off scenario. A lot of salespeople get on sales calls, cross their fingers and hope that it all works out. In fact, according to Spotio, 58% of buyers report that sales reps are unable to answer their questions effectively, and only 13% of customers believe a salesperson can understand their needs according to research conducted by The Brevet Group. This means while winging it may work every now and then, it isn't a reliable strategy.

Top-performing salespeople use a pre-call plan to increase their chances of success.

WHAT IS A PRE-CALL PLAN?

Pre-call planning is the preparation you do before a sales call to maximize the opportunity. There are endless ways to do a pre-call plan, but I'm going to share the process I teach my clients to give you a proven framework to build on.

But before we jump into how to do a pre-call plan, let's talk about why this is important.

More Prepared

Pre-call planning helps you think about the objective of the call and what you need to do beforehand to increase the chances of accomplishing that outcome. This preparation becomes crucial in decreasing the risk of miscommunication, especially when you have multiple people on both sides of the table.

In addition to the information gathered, a pre-call plan equips you mentally and emotionally for the call, allowing you to remain focused and emotionally objective.

Increased Confidence

When you're prepared, you feel more confident during the call because you already know your game plan and aren't making it up as you go. Plus, we all know that confidence is contagious. Your confidence in the questions you're asking and the information you're presenting makes your prospective client gain more trust and assurance in you as well. Lastly, by planning in advance, you can tailor your approach to meet the specific needs and expectations of your potential customer.

Time Management

Pre-call planning will help you manage your call more effectively because you know exactly what you need to cover in the allotted time.

I notice when I'm coaching sales professionals that this is a detail that is often overlooked. The salesperson will have a list of talking points they want to discuss without considering what's realistic given the amount of time they have. You don't want to cram an hour-long conversation into a 30-minute call just to check it off your list. Instead, ask for the time you both need to determine if it's a mutual fit. If your meeting is already scheduled, prioritize what you want to talk about given the amount of time you have.

Improved Outcome

By preparing in advance, you're more present, focused and effective during the call. This level of readiness can lead to a better outcome, such as increased sales and stronger relationships with your potential customers.

I have a client, Megan, who helps companies develop their retirement and benefits plans. Most of her business comes from advisors, who bring her in to assist with their clients, and one of the biggest challenges she was facing was that she was often being brought in *after* the advisor had already met with the prospect.

She would be given the end-client's information, and then would come to the second meeting with a proposal. As you can imagine, she was having a hard time converting because she wasn't getting all the information she needed from the advisors in advance. This forced her to try to build rapport with the end-client right before presenting the proposal, and then she was spending hours afterward redoing the proposal with the correct information.

When we started working together, the first thing we did was map out her sales process to include her either doing her own discovery call with the end client or a joint call with the advisor so she could gather the information she needed.

The second step was to create a pre-call plan that she could use with the advisor to ensure they were on the same page when they had joint calls. The very next opportunity that presented itself, they closed. Winning!

When I asked her what was different, she said that because she and the advisor met prior to the call, they were both aligned on the objective of the call, and she was able to pace herself and spend the right amount of time discussing her part of the deal versus being squeezed in at the end.

She was no longer going into the meetings blindly. Now, Megan knew what she wanted to communicate, and both she and the advisor had an understanding about the client and were able to better collaborate with the same end-goal in mind.

DIFFERENT TYPES OF PRE-CALL PLANS

There are two different types of calls you can do a pre-call plan for:

Prospecting calls: The prospect isn't expecting your call.

Sales calls/Appointments: A scheduled call.

The information you need to gather and what you need to do to properly prepare will vary depending on the type of call you're making.

Let's take a prospecting call, for example. The objective of your pre-call plan for a prospecting call is to gather enough information to customize your messaging and warm up the call. You can do this by researching the company, your point of contact, and seeing if you have any mutual connections on LinkedIn. The goal is to find at least one leverage point you can use to lower their guard, start a conversation, or pique their interest. Although we are talking about this in the context of cold calling, I've used this same approach in social selling as well.

There was a billion-dollar company that I had done some work for in a different division and capacity a couple of years prior, and I had my assistant find the point of contact on LinkedIn because I was interested in working with them again. I put together a personalized message that referenced the previous work I had done, what I do today, and how I might be able to help them. The point of contact responded, we set up a Zoom meeting, and it led to two contracts. What made this work was the preparation I did before, and the same is true when you're cold calling.

With an appointment, the process is more detailed because the prospect has already agreed to talk to you. We'll spend the rest of this chapter focusing on pre-call plans for appointments.

PARTS OF THE PRE-CALL PLAN

Pre-call plans work best when they are tailored, however, there are some universal pieces of information that you should include in your pre-call planning.

We'll divide the pre-call planning process into two phases: research and run-through.

Below are some questions you might want to consider when journeying through the two phases. You don't need to ask all of these questions. Pick the questions and pieces of information that are most relevant for you and your prospect.

RESEARCH

In this phase, you are focused on getting some background information on the company and the people that you are meeting.

Company: What industry are they in? Have they been in the news lately? Are they privately-owned or publicly traded? How big are they (revenue, headcount, locations)? How might size impact their buying process? Who are their competitors? What's their position in the marketplace?

Point(s) of Contact: Who's going to be on the call? What's their roles, titles, and responsibilities? How long have they been at the company or in their role? Are there any names that you're not sure how to pronounce? Do you have any mutual connections on LinkedIn?

Some of the information you research may be used explicitly during your sales call. For instance, if you noticed that you and one of the contacts went to the same college or that they recently joined the organization, you might mention that during the call, if it's relevant.

Other details you may use *implicitly* to determine what questions you want to ask, which projects you may want to reference, and objections that you want to eliminate upfront. Suppose you notice that they are a global organization. The projects you reference should be projects for other global organizations so they are confident that your company can handle a project of their size. On the other hand, if they are a small company with one location and a handful of employees, you should have similar projects to reference to show your ability to support small businesses.

Other Information: What information do you already have about them? Are they already in your CRM? Where did they come from (lead source)? Do you already know some of their pain points or why they're interested in meeting? Is there an incumbent that you need to be worried about? Are there any red flags, concerns, or potential issues that you want to address?

RUN THROUGH

Once you've completed your initial research, you will then use the information you've gathered to map out the call.

What's the purpose of the call and desired outcome?

I know this sounds obvious. The goal of the call is to close them, right?! While that may be true if you have a one-call close, that changes if you have, say an 18-month sales cycle. The goal of the initial conversation, in this case, isn't going to be to close them. The objective is likely to identify what they're currently doing, and to see if there is a problem that you can potentially solve. When thinking of the end-goal of the call, you want to consider two things: how much time do you have and where are you in the sales process. The goal for an initial call is quite different from the goal of a proposal meeting.

What questions do you want to make sure you ask?

Make a list of the questions you want to ask. The purpose of writing them down isn't that you necessarily go question-by-question or that you follow a script. Writing the questions down helps you to remember what you want to ask, and to give you something to go back and reference if you get stuck or forget.

What are some questions you think they may ask you?

This is a game-changer! Give some thought to the questions you may be asked and how you want to answer them. This will keep you alert so you're not caught off guard or stunned if they come up.

Potential Pain Points

Think of some of their pain points, and brainstorm questions that you can ask around them ahead of time to avoid the pressure of trying to do it in real-time.

Lastly, practice and rehearse the first two minutes of your call. We'll talk more about this is Chapter 8.

TEAM SELLING

Team selling is having more than one person from your organization on the call and this is when pre-call plans are most critical. Maybe it's you and the sales development rep who set up the call. You may have someone from operations or a subject-matter expert that's there to answer technical questions. Or it's possible that your sales manager or CEO may join for extra reinforcement.

It doesn't matter who that person is, you need to set up a joint pre-call plan before the day of the call. If there's any resistance with doing a pre-call plan, then get them a copy of this book and highlight this section for them!

Not having a pre-call plan is bad when it's just you on the call, but it's even worse when you have multiple people at the meeting who are not in sync or on the same page.

It's obvious when there's no pre-call plan because no one knows who's leading the meeting. Everyone looks at each other to figure out who is going to kick things off, and then eventually someone says, "Okay, I'll start." This is a terrible first impression to make with a potential client. It shows a lack of preparation and appreciation of their time. Another telltale sign is that people hesitate to ask questions because they don't want to derail the conversation or they're talking over each other, and the prospect feels like they're playing dodgeball with the questions. When you do team-selling, you need to define each person's role during the pre-call planning to eliminate any confusion.

A final point is that your prospect doesn't want to have to repeat themselves. Share the notes from any previous conversations and background information to make sure your team is up to speed prior to the meeting.

Is doing a pre-call plan *really* necessary?

One of the biggest pushbacks I get from salespeople (and you might even be thinking it) is that they don't have time to do a pre-call plan because their calendar is jammed packed with appointments and internal meetings. To that I say, "You don't have time not to do a pre-call plan."

Remember, buyers have access to more information than ever before. That means that they will likely research you, your company, your products, pricing, and alternative options (aka your competitor) before they ever have a conversation with you. So, if you're not doing a pre-call plan, it's going to show instantly in the questions you ask and you're going to find yourself behind the eight-ball. When you follow a practical pre-call plan process, it doesn't have to take a long time, but the time you do invest will pay dividends.

In case you're still concerned that you don't have enough time to do pre-call planning, here are three simple things you can do to add it to your to-do list.

Build your pre-call plan into your calendar. Set your calendar to automatically include a 15-minute buffer in between meetings so you have time to prep for your call.

Batch your pre-call planning. Put time on your calendar each day or each week, depending on what makes the most sense for you, to do all your pre-call planning at one time. I used to do this when I did a lot of prospecting. Fridays were my days to build out my prospecting list for the next week and to do all my initial research. This prep had me ready to hit the ground running on Monday.

Set a timer. It's easy to go down the research rabbit hole of over-researching or over-planning. To prevent this, set a timer and a specific goal to make it easier for you to stay focused while you're doing your pre-call planning. If you're researching for prospecting calls, give yourself 30 minutes to research six prospects, and find one major piece of information for each. On the other hand, you may have a targeted list and it takes you 15-30 minutes for each prospect. The key is to pick an amount of time that makes sense for you and stick to it.

SALES AND SOCKS

The second common pushback is the belief that pre-call plans are for amateurs and newbies. Wrong! Top-performing salespeople know that it's the fundamentals, not fancy techniques, that make them successful. It's mastering the classic John Wooden approach.

John Wooden coached the UCLA basketball team for 12 years. During his tenure, his team won the National Collegiate Athletic Association (NCAA) Championship 10 times; seven of which were consecutive. He is arguably one of the greatest coaches of all time.

On the first day of practice, the first lesson Coach Wooden went over with his team of elite basketball players was how to put on their socks and shoes properly. Why? Because he knew that his players were playing at a highly competitive level and if their socks weren't put on correctly, they would get blisters on their feet. Those blisters would slow them down and impact their ability to perform at an optimal level. A grown man taught a team of grown men how to tie their shoes properly so their laces wouldn't be too tight at the top of their feet causing discomfort. He taught them to tie them twice to keep them from coming undone and risking the chance of them either falling or stopping, which would break their momentum.

Your pre-call plan is the equivalent of Coach Wooden's socks and shoes principle.

When you skip the pre-call plan, you run the risk of:

- Not being prepared
- Being blindsided by questions
- Making a bad first (and last) impression
- Missing out on critical information because you haven't done your research.
- Skipping steps in the sales process
- Ruining a qualified opportunity

It's worth noting that a pre-call plan doesn't stop at the initial call. You should do some level of pre-call planning every time you're meeting with a prospect during the sales process. Each encounter doesn't have to be formal and can be simply jotting some bullet points and questions on a notepad. But you should always value your prospect's time and be intentional about what you want to get accomplished during the conversation.

Remember, "We'll see" isn't a reliable sales strategy.

It doesn't matter if the ink is still wet on your degree or if you've been in sales long enough that you remember using a Rolodex, taking 15-30 minutes to prepare for an appointment is part of the routine that top sales professionals follow.

Chapter 7

BUILD GENUINE RAPPORT

"Rapport is the foundation of all trust, and trust is the
foundation of all relationships."

Stephen M. R. Covey

What's the first word that comes to mind when you hear the word
rapport?

This is one of my favorite questions to ask when I'm training sales
teams on how to build rapport. It truly gives me so much insight
into their perspective of this powerful word.

Typically, they say things like:

- Mutual
- Trust
- Commonality
- Respect
- Relationship
- Connection

And according to Webster Dictionary, *rapport* can be defined as:

a relationship characterized by agreement, mutual understanding, or empathy that makes communication possible or easy.

What I really like about this definition is that it not only defines what rapport means and gives characteristics of rapport, but it also highlights the *outcome* of building rapport—easier communication. This detail is incredibly significant because many salespeople think sales is about having the best product, competitive price, or convincing pitch. However, at its core, sales is all about your ability to communicate effectively with other people.

The better you get at communicating, the more you will sell.

This brings us back to the last part of Webster's definition of rapport: that makes communication possible or easy. In other words, if you want to get better at communicating with potential clients, you want to make sure that you know what genuine rapport is and how to build it.

IT WAS NICE MEETING YOU!

You've met someone for the first time, and it felt like you've known them forever. You all were laughing, engaged, and tag-teaming the moment. Although you couldn't pinpoint what it was, you "got each other," and the conversation flowed so easily that before you knew it, minutes or even hours had flown by.

You've also been in social settings where you met someone for the first time, and you instantly knew it would be the last time. Once again, you may or may not know exactly what felt off, but something didn't click. You tried to push through the conversation, but it dragged on and on, and you couldn't help but look around for an escape.

Excuse me! It's time for a bathroom break!

What's the difference between those two interactions?

Rapport.

Rapport is established in seconds, relationships are built over time.

And if you don't know how to build rapport, you won't have the opportunity to build a relationship.

I recently interviewed a half-dozen instructional designers to help me redo some of my sales training courses. It's always interesting being the prospect because I can't help but dissect people's approach to selling. Within the first 30 seconds of the last instructional designer I interviewed, I knew that I wasn't going to hire her. Not only was she late to the call, but her demeanor was off-putting. Her arms were folded, she was curt in her communication, and she had an air of arrogance or at least that was my perception.

But here's the thing, based on her portfolio, she had the *most* experience, and she even asked the *best* questions, but she didn't get the project. I knew we would not work well together merely based on the level of rapport or lack thereof.

Top performing sales professionals know that your ability to build authentic rapport is a competitive advantage.

Now, when I talk about rapport this is where salespeople think they naturally excel, especially if they're friendly and outgoing. However, being extroverted or a people-person doesn't mean you're building true rapport. True rapport is when the prospect is open and honest with you, even if it doesn't seem like it's in your best interest.

Here are some signs that there's room to improve your rapport-building skills:

- Prospects seem disinterested or unresponsive during conversations.
- They're reluctant to share information regarding their goals, challenges, or budget.
- They mislead you (intentionally or unintentionally) about their decision-making process.
- They use your proposal or competitor's proposal to negotiate a better deal.
- They disappear or don't respond to multiple voicemails or emails.
- They don't want to answer any of your questions, they just want a price.

If you've ever experienced any of these, then you really want to pay attention to some of the strategies, tactics, and mindsets that can be holding you back from establishing a bond with your prospects.

WAYS TO BUILD RAPPORT

Your inability to sincerely connect with people will stop you from being able to earn enough trust to ask the deeper questions to properly qualify them and convert them. And in the event that you're able to do it once or twice, the larger the deal size that you're working on, the more important your ability to connect with people on a personal level becomes.

By the way, when I say, "personal level," I'm not talking about your family, favorite sports team, or hobbies. I'm talking about having empathy for the individual you're talking to and not solely concerned about the deal you're working on.

Notice how I keep saying genuine rapport—this is on purpose. The only thing worse than having no rapport is talking to a salesperson that is trying so hard to build rapport that it comes off contrived and forced, which happens far too often. Many confused salespeople believe that being friendly, outgoing, and extroverted means that you can build rapport.

Now there are several things that you can do to build rapport and there's different techniques that I teach my clients, but at the heart of building rapport is understanding that the purpose is to clear the path for communication.

Be genuinely interested in them.

To be genuinely interested in your prospect means that you really want to understand where they are today, what their current challenges are, what they've tried before and why it hasn't worked, and what it is that they're trying to achieve. And while gathering all of this information will help you put together a proposal, more importantly, it will help you understand where that person is, where their perspective is, and what their goals and ambitions are. When you put yourself in your prospect's shoes, the better questions you ask because you can imagine their fears, concerns, desires, and challenges as if they were your own.

A few years ago, I was working with a VP of sales, who had climbed the ranks from an individual rep to a sales manager, and now she was the organization's first VP of sales. As we were wrapping up our proposal meeting, she paused and thanked me for creating a safe space for her to be honest about what wasn't working in the sales department. She also mentioned that many of the things she shared with me she hadn't been able to share with anyone else, including my competition!

Have fun.

I think sometimes in sales we can be so overly serious and "professional" that we forget we're selling to other human beings. You don't sell to companies, corporations, or institutions. You sell to the people who work at companies, corporations, and institutions. Therefore, selling should be fun, so show your humanity. That doesn't mean you have to be a comedian and tell jokes, forcing humor. But it encourages you to be personable.

Relax. Read the room. Adapt your communication style to meet the needs of your prospect, all while still being true to who you are.

Ask the difficult questions that no one else has asked.

This is often the shot that most salespeople don't think to take because they're scared to ask the difficult questions out of fear that somehow it will kill a deal they don't even have. But the reality is that when you ask your prospect questions that they've never even thought about or you take a chance and address the elephant in the room, it *actually* deepens the rapport. This brave act shows your prospect that you're thinking about their business and their pain points from a different perspective.

It also shows that you're not afraid to talk about the challenging topics, whatever that may be in your world. I do this all the time with prospects (and clients), and it never ceases to amaze me how quickly it elevates the conversation, creating space to be honest about things that could potentially prevent the deal from closing anyway. I assume you're like me in that you much rather have the conversation upfront opposed to ignoring it, presenting a proposal, only to get stuck in proposal purgatory in the end.

Communicate with your whole self.

There are three different ways that we communicate with other people: the words we use, our tonality, and our body language.

When I'm doing training sessions on how to build rapport, I do an exercise where I put salespeople in small groups face-to-face, and I have them discuss how much of their communication they think comes from their words, body language, and tonality. The only two rules are that they must come to a consensus, and the total has to equal 100%.

As you can imagine, the numbers and explanations they come up with are as varied as the groups themselves. Some groups think words are the most important, while others think how you say something (tonality) is the most important. There's always one group that can't reach a consensus, and each person takes turns campaigning for their numbers. And I can't forget the group that thinks they're all equally important because they all work together.

MEHRABIAN'S COMMUNICATION THEORY

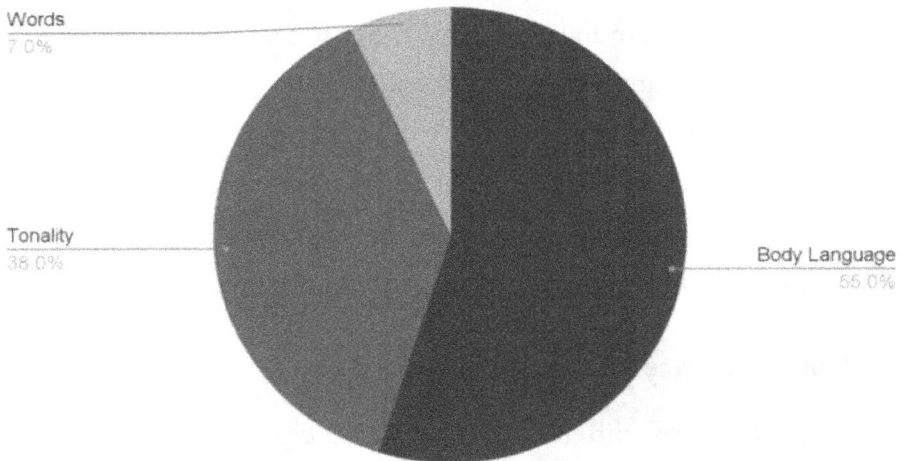

Words
7 0%

Tonality
38 0%

Body Language
55 0%

According to Albert Mehrabian, only 7% of the way that we communicate with other people is through the actual words that we use. This is always surprising for people, because they believe that words would rate higher. Now, of course, this doesn't mean that the words you use aren't important, but instead of focusing primarily on what you're saying, you also need to focus on *how* you're saying it, verbally and nonverbally.

Tonality is the second biggest factor in communication, coming in at 38%. Growing up, if you had a mom like mine that could say your name five different ways with five different meanings, then this makes perfect sense. Emotion is a big part of your voice and the tone you use, so think about how your tonality (which also includes pace, pitch, volume and cadence) is impacted when the prospect catches you off guard with an unexpected question. Or what about when they're pressuring you for a discount and you know you're behind on your numbers for the month.

There's a good chance you won't sound as confident as you'd like to in those tense situations.

And 55% of the way that you communicate with other people face-to-face comes through your body language like facial expressions, gestures, handshake, eye contact, smiling, and even the way that you dress. The important thing to note is that most of your body language happens subconsciously. You may be saying one thing with your mouth, but your body language could be saying something completely different.

Look at the relationship you're in now or that you've had in the past to see this nonverbal communication style at work. At some point, you have sensed that your significant other was upset or frustrated, but when you inquired about it, they likely told you some variation of "I'm fine" or "Everything is okay."

However, their folded arms, closed-off demeanor, quick-eye contact, and annoyed smirk reinforced that they were *indeed* not fine. They're body language was overriding their tone and words, and the same miscommunication can happen during a sales conversation. You may try to sound confident when you're reviewing the pricing during a proposal review, but your body language may show that you're uncomfortable. When you're doing your pre-call plan that we talked about in Chapter 6, don't just practice what you want to say, practice *how* you want to say it, too.

Remember, the 3-part communication pie helps you to communicate more effectively and build genuine rapport.

BUILDING YOUR RAPPORT BANK ACCOUNT

Rapport is like a checking account. If you have $500 in the bank and you try to withdraw $1,000, you're going to get declined for not having enough money to complete the transaction. When you use the tips and strategies, we've covered to improve your communication, it's like depositing in your personal rapport checking account. Your goal is to make enough deposits so that when you need to make a withdrawal, your account doesn't overdraft.

With that said, here are some common mistakes that keep you in the negative when building rapport with potential customers.

Not actively listening: Salespeople often make the mistake of talking too much and not listening enough to their customers. Active listening involves paying attention to what the customer is saying, staying in the moment, and being more interested in them than just selling your stuff.

Being insincere: Prospects can usually tell when someone is not being genuine or real. You need to be authentic in your interactions if you want to build trust. I'm sure you know how icky it feels when a salesperson lays it on too thick.

Focusing too much on the sale: Rushing to close the sale can come across as pushy and turn customers off. While it's important to make the sale, your first priority is knowing that if you fail to build rapport with people, they're not going to share their true pain points, budget, process, or any other information that you need to make your prospect a paying client.

Not adapting to the customer: Every customer may have a different communication style and preference. You want to be adaptable and able to adjust your communication style to fit the customer's needs and comfort level, while remaining genuine and relatable.

You can bank on the fact that working on your rapport building skills pays off in time, but authenticity and sincere connection are at the heart of it all.

Stay personable.

Address the elephant in the room.

Start the conversation.

And, most importantly, remind yourself that selling is establishing trust by using your words, tonality and body language to communicate with another human being.

Chapter 8

SET UP YOUR CALL

"Success is not about how hard you work, it's about
how smart you work."

Robert Kiyosaki

Most success principles go over people's heads because they're
counterintuitive. On the surface, they defy all logic and don't make
sense, which is exactly why they work.

In the personal finance space, they tell you to pay yourself *before*
paying your bills so you can build an emergency fund, save, or
invest. This is counterintuitive and may be illogical to grasp,
because most people are used to paying their bills and then trying to
save anything they might have left over, yet somehow it never seems
to be much.

In the health and wellness space, they tell you that sometimes you're
not losing enough weight because you're not eating *enough* calories
for your metabolism to function at its optimal level. This
contradicts the endless bowls of salads, bland chicken dinners, and

restrictive diets that most of us think about (or try) when working hard to shed a few pounds.

Well, the same is true in sales.

Some of the best principles are counterintuitive, like this one ...

If you want to get better at closing, you actually don't need to focus on improving your closing skills—at least not to start.

Here's the thing: Closing should be the easiest part of the sale because if you do everything right with your pre-call planning and execution on the call, "the close" shouldn't be a surprise for you or your prospects. When done correctly, "the close" is the natural next best step.

However, if you make some mistakes, you fail to have a consistent sales process, or you skip important steps along the way, then closing becomes a challenge and you're now having to pull out a bunch of tactics, hacks, and discounts to get the deal done.

So, what should you focus on instead of closing?

The Setup!

Your Setup is the first 5 to 10 minutes of your sales call, and you want to master this part because it helps you close out your call strong.

The amount of work you have to do at the back end of the deal trying to get it to close is 100% correlated to the work you didn't do at the front end.

In other words, if you're having to spend a lot of time and energy trying to get a deal over the finish line, it's probably because there's some steps you missed or questions you didn't ask earlier in the process.

Your mission is to set up your call for success early on, so closing the deal is easy.

NETFLIX AND SELL

When you're watching a new series or movie on Netflix, how long does it take you to determine whether you're interested?

If you're like me, within the first few minutes, you decide on whether or not you want to continue or return to the home menu and search for something else to binge.

Your prospects follow a similar process. The first 5 to 10 minutes of your sales call are vital and sets the tone for the rest of the conversation. If you deliver your Setup well, it opens the door to build rapport, uncover the pains and goals your prospect is experiencing, and gather additional information you need to see if your product or service is a good fit.

However, if you don't set up your call properly, then it will feel like you're pulling teeth trying to extract any information to help you help them. Their answers will be short, leaving you to try to fill in the gaps, which is never good.

So, here's the breakdown of The Setup.

The Setup consists of four elements:

- **Objective:** Why are we having this call?

- **Time:** How long do we have?

- **Outline:** What will we cover?

- **Outcomes:** What will potentially happen at the end of the call?

Before we dive into each one, keep in mind that you will do your Setup throughout the entire sales process: initial meeting, discovery, proposal, etc., but your Setup is best used when you have an appointment or a scheduled call that's at least 15 minutes. *I even use a modified version for client meetings because it keeps the conversation on track.*

Objective

The objective is the purpose or reason for the call.

While everyone's natural response is "to close" a sale, that isn't always the case. Depending on what you're selling and where you are in the sales process, the objective could be to identify if there's a pain point that's big enough for them to fix. Perhaps you need to get beyond the decision influencer to the decision maker, or to gather details necessary to design a pilot program that gives them a proof of concept.

I was recently talking to a sales rep, David, who was complaining that he had been working on an opportunity for over 18 months and he still hadn't been able to close the deal. He mentioned that he had another call coming up, and naturally, I asked him the purpose of the call. Without any hesitation, his knee-jerk reaction response was "To see if we can wrap up the deal." His track record wasn't convincing me that this approach would work, and after asking a couple of questions, we brainstormed a few other objectives that were more realistic, and could provide a visual of the process that could get him closer to the destination of possibly closing the deal.

Here's what we came up with:

Objective 1: Identify if there's still a need worth fixing.

Objective 2: If there is a need, identify why the deal is stalled.

Objective 3: If it is pricing related (it was a six-figure investment), ask if a pilot would be a better fit. If it's not pricing related, weigh the likelihood that roadblocks or red tape would be addressed.

Objective 4: Get a definitive timeline and agreement to next steps.

Objective 5: If you can't get an agreement, walk away.

Do you see how this is a much clearer and realistic path?

Now David could confidently structure his call based on the mini objectives. And he could decide, at any point, if it was better to walk away. These mini objectives were put in place to course-correct my client's sales process, but you won't need these when your one objective is clear. *This deal was already in progress before I started working with them, so we were having to backtrack and reset.*

As we discussed in Chapter 6: Creating a Pre-call Plan, the objective may or may not be shared with the prospect. If the objective is to do a site visit, it's perfectly fine to share that with the prospect. However, if the objective is to find out their pain points and potential budget, you're probably better off saving that for your outline. (You will learn more about this in just a second).

Time

The time is how long you have on the call.

We've all been there. You're halfway through a sales call, and you're finally getting to the good stuff. But before you can, the key person on the call interrupts you and says that they need to leave early, but they'll catch up with their colleagues or they'll read the notes. Instantly, your stomach drops, knowing the likelihood of the deal moving forward just went downhill.

To avoid this, you want to make sure that everyone is on the same page by confirming how much time you have at the beginning of the meeting. If someone needs to leave early, at least you will find this out before you start as opposed to in the middle of the call. As a result, you can make an educated decision on how you want to proceed.

Outline

The outline is what will be covered during the meeting.

The outline should include what they'd like to discuss during the meeting. This is a powerful tool because whatever your prospects say they want to talk about is likely a priority for them or a potential pain point. Furthermore, it allows you to manage expectations and control when you talk about certain topics during the call. A trap that salespeople find themselves in all the time is when the prospect starts asking questions about capabilities of your product or service before you've even uncovered the problem.

If you start answering these questions without context for why they're asking, you can talk yourself into a corner. Nevertheless, when you have an outline, it keeps you organized, and you can let them know that you'll be covering the specifications later in the conversation. Lastly, by sharing what you want to cover, you and the prospect can make sure you agree and that there's no hidden agenda.

Outcomes

The last part of your Setup is outcomes.

Simply put, tell your prospect what could potentially happen at the end of the call: we decide whether it's a fit, you sign the agreement, and we get started, we'll book a meeting with one of our subject-matter experts, we'll pull in additional people from their team, or we'll book a time to review the proposal together.

The outcomes that you mention should align with the purpose of the meeting and where you are in the sales process. A proposal meeting doesn't require you to mention looping in additional people. Instead, my outcome would be that we'll review the proposal together, and the prospect can decide to proceed as is, make some modifications, or amicably part ways.

Make sure your outcomes are clear, stated upfront, and agreed to by your potential client, so you can come back to them at the end when you're setting your next step.

When you do your Setup correctly you:

- Set clear expectations and ensure that you and your prospect are on the same page.
- Maintain control, while giving your prospect perceived control.
- Build connection and credibility.
- Identify what's important to them.
- Show that you are confident.
- Respect everyone's time, especially yours.
- Differentiate yourself from other salespeople.
- Make it easy to close the deal or clearly set your next step.

CLEAR NEXT STEP

After reviewing thousands of sales resumes and conducting hundreds of interviews, there is one thing that I found salespeople love to tout as one of their strengths that's actually a huge red flag for me.

Ready for it?!

"I'm really good at following up."

Yep, I know you're probably shocked by this because you've been taught for years that the money is in the follow up. I'll shed some light on whether this concept is true or not in just a second, but first let me give you some context.

One of the things I do as a sales consultant is participate in my corporate clients pipeline meetings. I can't tell you how many times I've sat in a pipeline meeting and within the first ten minutes a common trend starts to become obvious:

- There's no expected close date or next step.
- The expected close date has changed several times over the last thirty days.
- All the expected close dates miraculously fall on the 1st, 15th, or last day of the month.

All of these are indications that the salesperson is spending a lot of time "following up" with prospects instead of getting a clearly defined next step.

When you're following up, you find yourself sending emails (or smoke signals) that say...

"I'm just following up..."
"I wanted to check in..."
"I wanted to circle back around..."
"I wanted to get an update..."
"Just touching base..."

Sound familiar?

The drawback with follow up is that it's one-sided. The deal is a priority for you because you want to get it closed before the end of the month or quarter, but that doesn't mean it's urgent for your prospect, and that's a problem!

While you continue to check-in every couple of days, hoping that something has changed, sooner or later, you will run out of things to follow up on. But you don't want to walk away after already investing so much time, energy, and effort, and you refuse to take this lukewarm lead out of your pipeline.

Your intention to follow up wastes valuable time on deals with a low probability of closing when you could be working on high-quality opportunities.

So, the million-dollar question is: What do you do instead of following up?

Well, I'm glad you asked!

It's simple: Set clearly defined next steps.

That's it. Clearly defined next steps, unlike following up, are mutually agreed on between you and the prospect regarding what will happen next.

That provides peace and you don't have to worry about being too "pushy" or desperate to "touch bases" every other day because you (and your prospect) will already know what the further actions are.

And you want to make sure your clearly defined next steps have these three components for it to be effective:

1. Specific steps
2. Date/timeline
3. Agreement by both parties

A bonus is having another meeting scheduled or conversation on the calendar that has been accepted by them.

Specific Steps

Gaining clarity in your next steps comes from getting specific on which steps to take. When wrapping up your meeting, you want to discuss the exact action steps that will be taken by both parties to move the deal forward, unless one of you has decided that it's not a fit.

The prospective client may need to bring in additional people on their side. You may need to audit their current system/site/software or consult your team about putting together a formal proposal.

Whatever steps that need to be taken on both sides, must be plainly outlined, ensuring you and the prospect are on the same page. Most of the time only one party (you) is doing something, while the other person (your prospect) is focused on another task that distracts them from whatever you're selling.

The only time when you don't need to talk about next steps in the traditional sense is if you're in a one-call-close. Next steps for a one-call-close would be whatever happens in your sales process after they say yes. Maybe you send a purchase order (PO), they connect you to procurement or accounts payable, or you have an onboarding call to introduce them to the operations team.

A quick note: If there are more than three steps on each side, you want to group them into three major groups and then let them know you'll follow up with a detailed email. By limiting it to only three, you lessen the chance of them feeling overwhelmed and increase the chance of them to follow through with the tasks at hand.

Date or Timeline

What's the timeline on when these next steps are due? If your prospect needs to review the agreement internally and get it approved by their legal team, you want to ask how long that process typically takes. I've seen clients have agreements tied up in legal and procurement for weeks, sometimes even months depending on the size of the organization and the deal. This applies to your action steps, too. Be sure to let your prospect know how long it's going to take on your end.

You can also use that timeline to be proactive and set a date for your next conversation to escape the back-and-forth email hassle.

Note: A sales cycle that's less than a week means your next call could be the next day. Even if you have a short sales cycle, you still want to discuss the action steps.

Agreement by Both Parties

The last component is straightforward and that's getting a verbal agreement from the prospect regarding the next steps and the timeframe, which should be easy.

You will find out immediately if a prospect isn't serious about moving forward when you start setting up next steps and they start weaseling out of it. Let them. Find out their hesitation, and if necessary, let them off the hook. You don't want to arm wrestle someone into a fake "Yes," only to find out weeks later that they don't want to continue.

Now, keep in mind nothing is 100% airtight. But 80% is better than having nothing when you're in the follow-up trap.

As you can see, setting crystal clear next steps will help you weed out the indecisive prospects, saving you a ton of wasted time, exerted energy, and misplaced effort. Now you can take the next steps without worrying about being too pushy or too hands-off, because you have timelines that you both have thoughtfully agreed to.

Think about your Setup as your "Yin" and your Clear Next Step as your "Yang." One unfolds at the beginning of your sales call, and the other at the end, but they're both working together to create a harmonious interaction, and when you learn how to master both, magic happens!

Chapter 9

ASK BETTER QUESTIONS

"The most serious mistakes are not being made as a result of wrong answers. The truly dangerous thing is asking the wrong questions."

Peter Drucker

Have you ever been working a deal and you're convinced that you can help your prospect save time, money, effort, or energy, but for some reason, they decide not to move forward?

You scratch your head trying to figure out what happened:

Was it your price?
Did they go with a competitor?
Was there something you missed in your proposal?

After training 10,000 salespeople, there's a good chance you didn't seal the deal because you didn't uncover what I call the whole P.I.E. Uncovering the whole P.I.E. is the difference between "How soon can we get started?" and "Follow back up with us in six months."

THE HARSH REALITY

In today's selling environment, uncovering the prospect's "pain" isn't enough. We all have problems and situations that we complain about, seek out solutions for, and still don't pay for the answer.

Why?

Because pain is only *part* of the equation. Asking surface questions to get to their pain points is only going to give you low-quality answers. What's happening is that you're likely asking the same superficial pain questions as your competitors.

I've actually shadowed sales calls where the prospect jumped right into sharing their "pain points" because they'd already talked to three or four other salespeople and wanted to speed up the process.

I imagine this is going to become more common as buyers become more pressed for time. That means you have to find a way to stand out from the competition and get past the traditional "pain points." I put "pain points" in quotations to emphasize that most salespeople aren't even taught what the persistent or recurring issues are that their prospects are experiencing in their world nor which questions to ask to reveal them. As a result, they ask surface-level questions that bring some light to their surface-level problems, but the actual pain points are still unknown.

The secret to getting to your prospect's true desires is what I call uncovering the whole P.I.E.

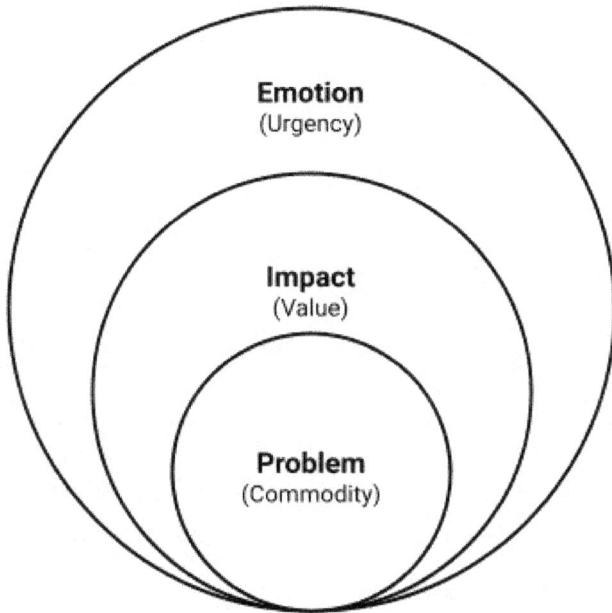

P - PROBLEM

The first piece of the P.I.E. is clearly identifying and getting to the root of your prospect's *problem*.

The problem is often what motivated them to reach out to you or what you discover when you contact them. If you sell recruiting services to small-to-midsize companies, your prospect might tell you that they've been having a hard time filling certain roles and are considering working with a recruitment firm.

Since the problem is what your prospect is most aware of, it's also the easiest thing for them to talk about.

And most salespeople believe it is their job to solve problems. The moment they hear these problems, they start selling them on how their company works to address the challenges mentioned.

However, when you sell at the problem level, you become a commodity and the only differentiator for commodities is price.

You want to get them talking about their problems, but you don't want to stay there.

Not only do you commoditize yourself when you start selling at this level, but it keeps your buyer in information mode and people don't buy when they're in information mode.

Also, notice the first slice of the P.I.E is called "problem," not pain and this is intentional. The terms are often used synonymously, but they're not the same thing.

IMPACT

Impact is the second part of the P.I.E. and building questions into your sales process helps you to expose the effect or *impact* of the problem or problems they're experiencing.

One day my kids and I were walking through our neighborhood, and we stopped at a bayou. My oldest son threw a rock into the pond. "Mom! Mom! Did you see that?!" he started screaming. "There's a fish in there." Spoiler alert: There's no fish in the pond. But what he saw was the ripple effect from him throwing the pebble into the water.

The same principle applies in sales. The ripple effect makes ripples in the water that are far bigger than the little pebble my son threw in, and whatever problem your prospect is facing causes a ripple effect that's much bigger than the original problem.

On the surface, it's likely that your prospect is so caught up in the day-to-day management of the problem that they haven't stopped to think about the ripple effect. On second thought, they may have thought about it, but didn't know how to fix it and have been living with the shortcomings until there's a tipping point where they must face reality.

Your job as a consultative salesperson is to ask the *right* questions to help your potential client identify and articulate the ripple effect of their problem. *Notice that I said, "their problem" and have placed the responsibility back on the client and not the sales professional.*

The amateur let-me-show-you-I'm-the-expert salesperson thinks they have to educate their prospects to demonstrate their expertise and value. However, when you know how to ask thought-provoking questions, you can get your prospect to self-discover the impact—a far more powerful strategy than trying to tell them what they're doing wrong.

I was doing a sales call with the CEO, sales manager, and COO of a recruiting company that's been around since the 1960s. My pre-call plan was done, and I had a list of questions I wanted to ask based on my initial research. About five questions in, the CEO interrupted himself as he was answering a question. "This sounds really ridiculous as I'm saying this aloud," he said. There was a long pause, and I reassured him that that's why my company exists.

It's possible that you're so used to following the same routine that you don't even realize how counterproductive it is until someone questions it. You need to be *that* person for your prospects.

And to be clear, the goal isn't to embarrass your potential clients. The objective is to ask them the type of questions they don't know to ask themselves. This will help them to make an informed decision on whether the issue is big enough to invest in. *(And I teach my clients how to do this without making their prospects feel incompetent or exposed.)*

Remember when I said problem and pain are not synonymous?

Here's why:

Problem + Impact = Pain

There is no pain without impact.

Using the same recruiting firm example from above, potential impacts could be:

- They're having to work longer hours because they're behind.
- The longer hours mean they're having to pay overtime.

- It's eating up too much of their time, which is impacting their ability to fill other roles.
- The team is feeling overworked and understaffed.
- The department heads are getting irritated because it's taking so long.
- If they're in a client-facing role, it can impact their ability to take on new projects or serve their current clients.
- If it's a leadership position, perhaps the team is operating without an official manager meaning other people are having to fill in, there are a lot of dotted lines, and it's causing friction or miscommunication.
- It's impacting customer service, sales, revenue, retention, or the ability to grow.
- They're having to "settle" on the people they hire, and it's taking longer for them to ramp up.

You can quickly see the difference between just talking about the problem and tackling it by asking questions that reveal the hidden impact that it's causing the larger organization. Problem is logical whereas impact focuses on the additional problems that "the initial problem" has created.

The impact level is where value is created.

There are six common external impact areas that are typically focused on when it comes to the team or organization. As you review the six areas, highlight the areas that are most applicable to your prospects.

Time	Delays, opportunity costs, responsiveness, time constraints, stress
Money	Pricing, revenue, profits, compensation
Efficiency	Turnaround time, wasted resources, higher costs, quality issues
Growth	Market share, capital investments, expansion, scaling, missed opportunities, flat or decreasing growth
Team	Morale, culture, collaboration, communication, leadership, layoffs
Operations	Supply chain, redundancy, bottlenecks, systems, processes, risks, production

You don't manufacture impact.

You can try to manufacture impact but let me warn you: *people's guards or BS radar will turn on in a flash, and you will start to get resistance*! Instead, top-performing salespeople are determined to ask the right questions to assist the prospect in seeing the impact for themselves, so they have a full understanding of what's happening, and they can decide whether it's important enough for them to do something about it.

EMOTION

The final piece of the P.I.E is emotion or personal impact.

While we would love to think that we are rational beings, numerous studies show that most decision-making is actually determined by our emotions. A poll by Gallup found that up to 70% of our decision-making is based on emotion, while the remaining 30% is based on rational, logical factors.

As the famous neuroscientist Antonio Damasio said, "We are not thinking machines that feel, we are feeling machines that think."

Salespeople usually think prospects are buying based on logic or thinking, but that's inaccurate.

People buy based on feelings and emotions, and then they use their logic or thought process to justify the decision their emotions made.

Identifying the emotion tells you how your prospect *feels* about the problem and how it is affecting and impacting them personally. Unfortunately, not enough salespeople get to this level, because they're already trying to sell at level one or two.

But the mindset of top-performing salespeople is knowing that this is the level where urgency happens. When you uncover the emotion or personal impact on the person you're talking to, it naturally creates an "act now" feeling, and you don't have to try to push the prospect into a "Yes."

Here's a quick story to drive home the lesson.

Our A/C went out on New Year's Eve in 2018, and it got down to 60 degrees in our house. We called out an A/C company, and they replaced the indoor and outdoor units. Unbeknownst to us, they didn't replace the panel that controls the air conditioning system. Fast forward to 2020, and our two-year-old unit started going out every few months. We called to schedule a time for them to look at it, but surprise, surprise––they had gone out of business!

My husband became an overnight handyman and would climb into the attic, press a few buttons, and voilà, the unit would come back on. That quick fix didn't last, and the unit went out again right when I planned to call an A/C company to come and check it out. But before I could, an A/C rep from another company unexpectedly knocked on our door and told my husband about their monthly maintenance plan and how he could have a tech come out the following day. The technician looked at our system, and he told us that the control panel was kaput. He then gave us two options.

Option 1: He can rewire the system and have both the upstairs and downstairs run off one thermostat. It would be a couple hundred bucks, and he can get it done the same day. The only disadvantage is that there would be a slight difference in temperature between upstairs and downstairs, and I wouldn't be able to control the upstairs.

Option 2: We could replace the whole control panel, but he would have to come back the next day. This option was four times as much, but I would be able to control the upstairs and downstairs separately.

My husband called me and presented both options. He wanted to go with the least expensive option #1 and have the technician do it right away. I, on the other hand, chose option #2, the more expensive one.

Why? Because I'm the spouse, who wakes up in the middle of the night when we have guests visiting in the winter, to make sure they are comfortable and not getting too hot upstairs when we have the heat on.

He doesn't!

So, the thought of not being able to control the thermostats separately was more painful to me (personal impact/emotion) than the additional money we would have to pay. The payoff for my husband was not high enough because there's no personal impact to him.

Now, let's revisit the recruiting company for you to clearly see how emotion plays a part in the impact.

- The person is frustrated and overwhelmed because they're having to work more hours trying to fill the roles.
- Their compensation and bonuses are tied to fulfilling roles.
- They're scared they will look incompetent and lose the trust of their direct reports and higher-ups.

- The problems are preventing a promotion within the organization.
- They're stressed and dread meeting with department heads.

Uncovering the whole P.I.E. isn't for you.

Of course, you benefit from presenting the whole P.I.E to your prospect, but it's to give them a 360-degree view of what's precisely going on in their business. This revelation not only shows your prospect that you are indeed the expert without having to say, "I'm the expert," but it also brings you awareness of the gaps and gives you the permission to advise your prospect more effectively on how to close them.

Yes, uncovering the whole P.I.E. is pleasing, but the P.I.E isn't for you, it's to satisfy your prospect.

Problem	Problem + Impact = Pain	Problem + Impact + Emotion
Awareness	Value	Urgency

Now, I know you may be thinking, L'areal, I love everything you just said, but how do I practically slice the whole P.I.E.?
The answer is simple: ask better questions.

The quality of your questions determines the quality of answers that you get.

So, if you're asking low-level questions, you'll get low-level answers.

It's that simple.

High-quality questions allow your prospects to think about their business or organization in a different way than they were thinking before. Why? Because when you dig deep enough to get your prospect thinking differently, you don't have to tell them you're different. *They'll know you're different.*

If your prospect can answer every question off the top of their head that means you're likely asking the same questions as the three other salespeople they've been talking to, and you need to dig deep and elevate the questions you're asking.

Here are some examples of P.I.E. questions to include throughout the sales process.

Problem:
- Can you walk me through what's happening?
- When did you first notice that?
- How long has that been going on?

Impact:
- Let's pretend we worked together, what would you like to see (# months) from now to say it was worth it?
- If we were able to (resolve the issue) how would that impact the (bottom line, speed to market, morale, or any relevant topic)?

Emotion:
- How does this impact you personally?
- What does success look like?

Obviously, the exact questions and wording needs to be customized to fit your world or industry, but you can see the difference between the questions and how they build on each other.

UNLOCK YOUR NEW SUPERPOWER

Superman has superhuman strength and heat vision. Spiderman can climb walls and sling webs. Black Panther has a vibranium suit that gives him added strength, speed, and martial art skills. And you have a new superpower: knowing how to ask high-quality questions.

Now, with great strength, comes great responsibility.

Asking high-quality questions is two-fold. You're able to ask better questions that build trust, credibility, and separates you from any competition, regardless of pricing. And, your questions will help your potential client truly understand their problem, how that problem is affecting their life or business on a much bigger scale, and determine with confidence that you are the person to solve it. Always remember, you create value based on the information you get, not the information you give.

For a free list of 20 high-quality P.I.E questions, visit www.PieQuestions.com

Chapter 10

DEBRIEF YOUR CALLS

"The only real mistake is the one from which we learn nothing."

Henry Ford

Have you ever finished a sales call and wondered what could have gone better? Maybe you stumbled on a particular question, or could it be that the client seemed uninterested when you walked through your proposal, and you didn't know why.

There's a good chance you recognized that something was "off" in the moment, but how often do you take the time to analyze the call to figure out what went wrong, and what you could do better in the future?

If you're like most average salespeople, the answer is rarely, if ever.

In sports, they call this process watching the film or the tape. By watching the film, players can analyze what happened during a particular play and what they could have done differently. They draw conclusions and then use their findings for player development and to prepare for the next game.

In sales, we call this process debriefing.

Proactively and consistently debriefing your sales call is a crucial opportunity to improve your skills, close more deals, and make more money.

Debriefing is the process of reflecting on what worked and what didn't during a conversation with a potential client.

Unfortunately, most salespeople never stop to debrief their sales calls, and they continue to make the same mistakes because they don't even know they're making mistakes. Instead, they blame the prospect for not getting the results they want, or they chalk it up to luck when they do. The problem is that you can't control "luck" or your prospect. The only thing you can control is you.

WHY DEBRIEF

Recognize your Behaviors and Subconscious Pattern

When you debrief correctly, you start to recognize your behaviors and subconscious patterns that are creating a particular outcome. I was doing a call debrief with a client, and she couldn't figure out why people kept telling her that they couldn't afford her company's services.

As we reviewed her calls together, it was clear that she wasn't asking enough questions to identify a big enough gap in their business. And since she wasn't asking enough questions, she was dominating the conversation with her background and her mission—neither of which is convincing enough for someone to buy. After listening to her calls, it wasn't surprising that she was getting resistance, because no one spends money to fix a problem they don't even know they have.

But here's the real eye-opening part. Prior to us reviewing the calls together, she kept blaming her prospects for being too cheap to invest in their business. In reality, her sales approach was causing the pushback.

Once she realized that, we mapped out a new sales process that included the right questions, and she started closing sales at even higher prices.

The dollars are in the debrief.

Improve Your Performance

Debriefing allows you to identify areas where you need improvement. By studying the call, you can pinpoint specific moments where you could have done better. You may notice that you didn't ask enough questions to fully understand the client's needs so they didn't see how your product or service could help them. On the contrary, maybe you talked too much and didn't give them a chance to speak so there wasn't an opportunity to build rapport.

Likewise, you might realize there was something that worked well on a call that you want to continue doing. By recognizing these areas, you can make changes in your future calls, improving your chances of closing more deals.

Get to The Root

We all make mistakes, but the value comes in when you learn from them. By debriefing your sales calls, you know the errors that were made, and you can start to understand what caused them.

Did you not prepare enough for the call?

Were you not confident enough in your presentation?

Were you nervous because it was a large deal?

Understanding the underlying reason behind the mistakes will teach you a great deal about yourself, your triggers, and your subconscious beliefs. This level of self-awareness prevents the same mistakes from happening in the future.

Better Understand Your Clients

The better you understand your prospective clients, the better you can help them, right? By debriefing, you gain an understanding of how they describe their problem and goals, and their responses to your questions, and you will then find out:

- Their needs and concerns
- Their communication style
- How they make decisions
- What's most important to them

Understanding their needs and concerns demonstrates that you genuinely care about their success while differentiating yourself from the competition. This approach builds trust and rapport, which can ultimately lead to more sales. However, you will miss out on this "play" if you're not "watching the tape" or in this case, debriefing your calls.

Address Potential Issues Sooner Rather Than Later

There have been times when I'm debriefing a discovery call, and I thought about questions I still needed to ask or things I needed to clarify before presenting the proposal. Depending on what the information is, I've called the prospect to ask those additional questions and get clarity before our proposal meeting. Other times, I've asked the questions at the beginning of the proposal meeting and made any adjustments in real-time. Either way, it gives me (and you) additional information to leverage while continuing to take them through the sales process.

Take the Emotion Out

Lastly, when you're working on a sales opportunity, it is easy to get emotionally involved. And when you get emotionally invested in a potential client, you may forget the process and start making avoidable mistakes. Debriefing your interactions with prospective clients after every single sales call will help you determine at what step in the sales process, you're likely to get attached. Also, understanding "why" will help you create a plan and "brace yourself" for the next call, and better control your emotions and focus on the process.

DEBRIEFING QUESTIONS

To get the most value out of your debrief, here are three simple questions I teach my clients to ask. You can always add more questions, but this is a fundamental framework to get you started.

- What worked or went well?
- What didn't work or did not go well?
- What will you do differently next time?

Let's break down each of these questions and give more context as to why they are necessary, and how they can position you to make a lot of money, if you use them consistently.

What worked or went well?

The purpose of this question is for you to recognize everything that went well during the call, no matter how big or small. Maybe you did a good job building a connection at the beginning or you asked a good open-ended question that got the prospect talking. You can even pat yourself on your back for sharing your value proposition or uncovering how they make decisions when purchasing products or services like yours.

Whatever you did well, it's critical that you recognize that and continue doing it.

You will be tempted to jump to questions two or three when you start debriefing, but the order of the questions has purpose. You always want to start with what you did well, even if you feel like you completely botched the call. Beginning this strategy with the positive keeps you open to introspection and reflection.

I have found that when you skip to questions two and three, you become overly self-critical, and it's easy to shift from a mindset of development and growth to a mindset of discouragement and groaning. Neither one of those will lead to a positive outcome or better results, so trust the process and acknowledge the good first.

What didn't go well?

After reflecting on your list of everything you did well, you now want to shift gears and think about what did not go as well on the call. Whatever you believe you could do better or wish you would've done, write it down or make a mental note of it.

If you want to take it a step further, you can use some of the exercises from Chapter 1: Master Your Mindset, to identify the beliefs that may have caused you to handle the call the way you did. Remember this isn't about beating yourself up, this is about recognizing areas of development. The more you become aware of the areas, the easier it is to improve.

Plus, no one runs a call 100% perfect—not even me.

When I debrief my calls, there's *always* at least one thing that I would different, even if I closed the sale.

Top-performing salespeople are continuously trying to get better!

What will you do differently?

While debriefing your calls when you're solo is productive, the process becomes even more powerful if you're doing team-selling. Whenever you're working with a sales development rep or a subject-matter expert, it's imperative that you debrief if you have more than one person on your team involved.

Immediately after your sales call, schedule in time to meet while the call is still fresh, and it's easier to remember what was shared. Plus, you're able to implement those lessons learned immediately and increase your chances of following through. There have been times when I realized I forgot a piece of information after I did my debriefing, and I called or emailed the prospect to get the details that I needed. Most debriefs should take no more than 5 to 10 minutes, depending on whether you're debriefing by yourself or as a team.

What my clients like most about these three questions is that they can be used for anything. In addition to using them to debrief sales calls, you can use them to debrief trade shows, networking events, conferences, client onboarding, training, or your goals. The possibilities are endless.

What did you notice about these questions?

Answer: All of these questions focus on YOU, and this is not by accident.

Many times, when I'm debriefing calls with salespeople, they tell me everything that the prospect did or didn't do.

"They took control of the call and wouldn't let me ask any questions."

"They told me they were the decision maker, but then I found out they were trying to sell it to their boss."

"They said that they really liked what we presented, but then they went with someone else.

Or, if it's later in the sales process ...

"They told me they didn't have a specific budget, but then complained that the price was too high after I presented the proposal."

While there might be some truth to these statements, the problem is that you can't control what other people do. You can only control what YOU do, and you have the ability to influence what other people do. That's why your debrief only focuses on what you could have said or done differently, and not what the prospect did or did not do, said or did not say.

With that being said, you should most definitely pay attention to what the prospect said or did in order to proactively think about what *you* need to do differently the next time this conversation may come up on a call.

Just remember that no matter what happens, you must take ownership for the outcome.

Here's how those statements are different when you're focused on you vs. the prospect:

Instead of ...	It becomes...
They took control of the call and wouldn't let me ask any questions.	I let them take control of the call. I should have taken control by pausing, resetting expectations, or asking a question.
They told me they were the decision maker, but then I found out they were trying to sell it to their boss.	I only asked about the decision maker instead of having them walk me through their internal process to get this signed off and funded.
They told me they didn't have a specific budget, but then complained that the price was too high after I presented the proposal.	I could have given them a range based on the initial conversation to see how they reacted before having my team spend hours putting together a detailed proposal.

Even if you don't know exactly what you should have done differently, it increases your awareness of what happened when you reflect.

I know I've spent a lot of time talking about debriefing calls that didn't go well, but you can (and should) debrief calls that *do* go well because they can boost your confidence and self-esteem as a sales professional.

I recently had a client, Melanie, close a $350,000 deal in less than a month, and their typical sales cycle is 45 days. What was interesting is that this account executive also had much smaller deals that were weeks past the expected closed date, and every time we did our calls, she had a reason why she still had her fingers crossed.

During one of our coaching sessions, we debriefed this large deal, and I asked her what was distinct about this deal in comparison to smaller deals that were taking longer to close.

Here are some of her observations as a result of debriefing:

Large Deal That Moved Fast	Small Deals That Were Stuck
• She was talking to the right person in the organization. • There was not only a need, but there was urgency, because they had an internal deadline to meet. • The pain of not moving forward and missing their internal deadline was greater than the additional money they had to spend to get the deal done.	• She was talking to someone with low influence in the decision-making process, so they were trying to sell it internally first. • The decision maker wasn't feeling the personal impact (emotion). • They were already using an alternative solution that was less expensive. • There was no immediate need.

This chart comparison of the two deals allowed her to come up with a strategy for her deals that were stuck, and she now sees and knows the criteria and roadblocks to look out for in upcoming sales calls.

None of this would have been possible without debriefing.

Unlike some of the other strategies and tools we've discussed, there's no ramp-up time to start debriefing. Start right now using the last sales call you had.

I guarantee you'll have at least one takeaway that will 100x the investment you made in purchasing this book.

You're welcome!

Chapter 11

WHAT'S NEXT?

"We know what we are, but know not what we may be."

Hamlet, Act IV, Scene 5

Over the course of this book, I've shared 10 advanced tactics that separate top-performing salespeople, who consistently hit their numbers regardless of the circumstances, from average or struggling salespeople. Here's a recap of what we've covered:

1. Master Your Mindset
2. Set Goals That Stick
3. Know Your Numbers
4. Keep Your Pipeline Full
5. Follow a Sales Process
6. Do a Pre-Call Plan
7. Build Genuine Rapport
8. Set-up Your Call
9. Ask Better Questions
10. Debrief Your Calls

Honestly, when most people complete a book like this, they're on an emotional high after being presented with such forward-thinking sales techniques that will refine their overall performance, and they can't wait to implement it. But in a few days, that excitement fizzles away, the motivation fades, and they're back to chasing the next shiny object.

It's a syndrome that many well-intentioned individuals suffer from because there are four levels of learning you have to go through to go from knowledge to habit. Decades ago, insurance trade group, LIMRA created the acronym K.A.S.H. to explain these four levels: Knowledge, Attitude, Skills, and Habits.

After conducting hundreds of sales trainings and coaching sessions, I've taken the four levels and put my own spin on K.A.S.H.

Knowledge

Knowledge is the first level of learning, and unfortunately this is where 90% of people who read this book will stay.

At this level, it's all about soaking up information, and there's no doubt that you learned some valuable content in the pages of this book. You probably got a different perspective on sales jargon that you've heard before or a reminder about behaviors you used to have when you first started your sales career.

Knowledge is power. But you and I both know that taking notes and getting new ideas alone won't supernaturally increase your sales.

The only way to get a different result is by taking different actions, and that brings me to the next level of learning.

Application

In my version of K.A.S.H., the second level of learning is application. This is where you put your pen down or close out your notes app and start taking action. As you apply what you have learned, you'll figure out what works for you, what doesn't work for you, and what modifications you need to adjust for the concepts in your world to make sense. This process is what we call the learning curve or the "messy middle," because things get ... well, messy.

You'll make mistakes. You'll skip some steps. And it's all part of the process, but beware. This is also where you will feel the impulse to go back to your old habits and you really want to challenge yourself to push *through* the learning curve, so you can get new results and develop transferable skills.

Skills

The "S" in K.A.S.H. stands for skills.

When you've practiced enough, you start to develop competency and it no longer feels as awkward when you use certain tactics and strategies.

Practicing and rehearsing your skills consistently replaces old habits, and you no longer have to think about it. Your abilities have now become a new, natural tendency, bringing us to the final level of learning.

Habit

A habit is something you do regularly, without making a conscious effort. Your newfound skills have become your new normal behavior. Habits are what create sustainable change and results, and to get to this level, you want to focus on failing fast. You read that right. Try "the thing," make the mistakes, course-correct, and then try again and again until you develop the best practices that all top-performing sales professionals adopt.

What's Next?

Throughout this book, I have shone a light on the strategies, mindsets, and habits that set top-performing salespeople apart from the rest, and it is my hope that each chapter has removed the uncertainty and frustration that you may have felt in the past with your sales performance. As we conclude, know with confidence that you now possess the knowledge and proven action steps necessary to become a motivated, top-performing salesperson.

However, the real test lies in your commitment to applying this knowledge, embracing the habits, and consistently taking action. Always remember that success in sales is not solely about achieving quotas or closing deals. It's about making a positive impact on your clients, building lasting relationships, and continuously improving yourself.

Recognize that the pursuit of sales excellence is a never-ending journey.

Embrace the idea that there is always more to learn, new challenges to conquer, and greater heights to reach.

Continually adapt, innovate, and evolve to stay ahead in an ever-changing sales landscape.

You have the power to become an exceptional sales professional who stands out from the crowd and is committed to making your mark.

The journey begins now!

WORK WITH ME?

Speaking

L'areal is available to speak in person, virtually, and hybrid. For more information about booking L'areal to speak at your next event or sales meeting, visit www.LarealLipkins.com/speaking

Training and Consulting

Interested in having L'areal work with your sales team? Need help auditing your sales processes? L'areal can create customized training and consulting options based on your team's needs.

To start the conversation, set up an introductory call with L'areal by visiting **www.LarealLipkins.com** and selecting "Book a Call."

Bulk Orders

Quantity discounts are available for orders of at least 100 books. To place a bulk order, email **Lareal@LarealLipkins.com** with the subject line "Bulk Order."

ABOUT THE AUTHOR

L'areal Lipkins is an expert on B2B sales, modern consultative selling, and sales process.

Before starting Lipkins Consulting Group, LLC, a sales training and consulting firm, she spent nearly a decade as a certified sales trainer for the largest sales training company in the world. During that time, she became fascinated with understanding why some salespeople succeeded while others struggled.

She quickly noticed that there are specific behaviors, skills, and mindsets that catapult high-performing salespeople into great levels of success and teaches tangible strategies that salespeople can use to close more sales immediately.

L'areal has trained over 10,000 sales professionals at companies like Indeed, Oracle, Aflac, Girl Scouts of America, St. Jude Children's Research Hospital, Wells Fargo, Multiview, Sanguine BioSciences, and dozens of small businesses all over North America.

As a speaker and trainer, L'areal is known for her dynamic, engaging, and practical approach to sales. L'areal is a top-rated speaker for Vistage, Entrepreneurs Organization (EO), Radio Advertising Bureau (RAB), and the National Sales Network. She has also been featured on numerous podcasts and media outlets, including Yahoo, Thrive Global, and Fast Company.

As a consultant, she specializes in helping companies build and optimize their sales process. As a result, they have a repeatable process that helps them shorten the sales cycle, ramp up new hires faster, close more business, and increase revenue profitably.

L'areal has a bachelor's in marketing from the University of North Texas and an MBA from the University of Texas at Dallas. She is also certified in Extended DISC and a certified Objective Management Group partner.

Today, L'areal spends much of her time speaking on stage, training sales teams, and working with companies to optimize their sales process. When L'areal is not working, she's hanging out with her husband and two sons in Houston.

ACKNOWLEDGMENTS

No one writes a book alone – it takes a team.

To my husband, who listens to, nurtures, and encourages all my random ideas (like writing a book or quitting my job to start my own sales consulting company), thank you! Without your support, it would be impossible for me to do what I do.

To my kiddos, thank you for allowing me to be more than just a mom. I get to be L'areal, and sometimes that means sharing me with clients and my team. I know one day you'll understand that every sacrifice I made was for you all. I love you!

To my VA, Laveet, thank you for helping me research, organize, and stay on track with this project. I know I'm a lot to manage! Thank you for your patience and grace, always.

To my editor, LB, thank you for finding all 3,000 changes (not an exaggeration) I needed to make before getting this book into people's hands. You're amazing at what you do, and I appreciate you ensuring my message was clear, cohesive, and impactful.

To my partner-in-crime, Brisa, where do I even begin? Your feedback and encouragement through this process have been amazing. Our lives are hectic, and I appreciate you finding time to read parts of the book while running your business, serving clients, and showing up for your family. Your friendship is priceless.

Thank you to my clients who trust me to train their teams, build their sales processes, and grow their businesses.

To every salesperson I've had the honor of training and coaching— You are the real MVPs! Every day you put your ego on the line to serve your clients, sell on behalf of your company, and earn a living to take care of your family. You keep the lights on and generate revenue that provides jobs for other people.

Seeing your wins is what keeps me going!

www.ingramcontent.com/pod-product-compliance
Lightning Source LLC
Chambersburg PA
CBHW032330210326
41518CB00041B/2058